# NEW

# Total English

## INTERMEDIATE

**Workbook** with Key

Antonia Clare and JJ Wilson
with Anthony Cosgrove

# Contents

# 1 Friends

## Vocabulary | friends

**1** Complete the sentences with the words and phrases from the box.

> a good sense of humour    best friend    colleagues
> ex-girlfriend    friend of a friend    get to know her ←conocerla
> have a lot in common    keep in touch
> lost touch    on the same wavelength
>
> en la misma onda

1 It has been really nice seeing you again. Let's try and _____ . Shall I call you next week?
2 She always makes me laugh. She has _____ .
3 Our relationship has finished so she's my _____ now. I think she's got a new boyfriend.
4 I've met him once or twice at parties. He's a _____ .
5 I'd like to _____ better because she seems very friendly. But I don't know her very well.
6 I'm going out on Friday with a few _____ from work.
7 Mario and I have a good relationship because we like the same things. We _____ .
8 Luis and I really understand each other very well. We're _____ .
9 I speak to Lucy every day on the phone. She's my _____ .
10 Unfortunately we _____ when we left university. I haven't seen him for years.

**2** Complete the adverts with the correct prepositions.

> *Are you interested* (1) _____ *books?*
> Would you like to spend time with friends talking (2) _____ books you have read?
> *Join us at the* BOOK CLUB *every Friday.*

> ● Do you worry (3) _____ your weight?
> ● Are you keen (4) _____ exercise but not good (5) _____ team sports?
>
> Join **Solutions Fitness Centre** and we'll help you feel better.

## Grammar | auxiliary verbs (*do, be, have*)

**3** **a** Put the words in the correct order to make questions.

1 Are/sports?/at/good/you
2 brothers/any/got/or/Has/sisters?/he
3 are/How/they?/old
4 you/German?/Do/like/studying
5 America?/been/Have/you/to
6 today?/you/seen/Have/boss/your
7 you/shops/Did/go/yesterday?/the/to

**b** Write short answers to the questions in exercise 3a. Use auxiliary verbs where possible.

**4** **a** Make questions from the prompts.

1 What/sports/you/interested in?
2 You/been/skiing/recently?
3 She/like/listening to/music?
4 Mozart/play/the violin?
5 Your parents/enjoy/the concert/last night?
6 Clara/had/her baby yet?
7 You/born/in Turin?
8 You/speak to Frances/yesterday?

**b** Match the answers (a–h) with the questions (1–8) in exercise 4a.

a) Yes, she does. She's really keen on Mozart.
b) No, I wasn't. I was born in Rome.
c) Yes, I did. She called me last night.
d) Yes, they did. They loved it.
e) Yes, he did. He taught himself when he was five years old.
f) I love skiing and watching football.
g) Yes, she has. He's called Jack.
h) Yes, I have. I went to Switzerland last week.

> Want to be fluent (6) _____ English, but don't want to spend all your money (7) _____ a language course?
>
> Join the **English Language Club**.

# Pronunciation | intonation in echo questions

**5** **a** Match the statements (1–8) with the replies (a–h).

1 Jenny and I are getting married.

2 I've just seen someone famous.

3 Bob's just a friend of a friend.

4 I don't want any dessert after that big meal.

5 My grandfather once played professional football.

6 My mobile phone has broken again.

7 It's my stepmother's birthday next week.

8 I fell out with my boss last year.

a Did he? That's amazing!

b Have you? Who was it?

c Did you? And how do you get on now?

d Has it? Do you want to use mine?

e Is he? I thought you knew him really well.

f Don't you? But I made it especially for you!

g Is it? What are you going to get her?

h Are you? Fantastic – when is the big day?

**b** 🔘 2 Listen and check.

**c** Listen to the eight dialogues in exercise 5a again. In which dialogue does the second speaker sound ...

• friendly and interested (FI)?

• bored (B)?

• annoyed (A)?

1 ___ 2 ___ 3 ___ 4 ___ 5 ___ 6 ___ 7 ___ 8 ___

# Reading

**6** Read the article and choose the best title, 1, 2 or 3.

1 Young people – are they big spenders?

2 China – the richest country in the world?

3 Shenzen – a changing city: how people spend their money

**7** Read the article again. Mark the sentences true (T) or false (F).

1 How you spend your money does not depend on how old you are.

2 The city of Shenzen has become richer because professional people have moved there for work.

3 People now spend twice as much money on education as before.

4 Most families in Shenzen have a mobile phone.

**8** What do the words in **bold** in the article mean?

1 This (line 13)      2 They (line 20)

    a China          a houses

    b education     b people

    c 1,000 yuan    c apartments

It's no surprise that what you spend your money on depends on your age, where you live, how big your family is, and how much money you earn. But have you ever thought about how people change their
5 spending when a whole city starts to get richer?

Shenzen, in China, has attracted lots of talented professionals in the last few years, and the average man or woman there now earns more than in any other medium-sized city in China. So what do these
10 Shenzen residents tend to spend their money on?

The first thing is education. This is very expensive in China, and professional people generally spend more than 1,000 yuan each on education. **This** is one and a half times more money than they spent
15 in 1995. They also spend four times as much on communications and telephones. In every one hundred households there are now ninety-three mobile phones and fifty-four home computers. People have started to buy bigger houses.
20 **They** now usually have an average five square metres more space in their apartments, and some have even bought second houses too.

The biggest change, however, has been in the number of people buying cars. In 1995 only four or
25 five families in every one hundred owned a car. Now this number has shot up, and there are well over one million cars in Shenzen.

## Vocabulary | personality

**1** Choose the correct word in *italics* to complete the sentences.

1 She's really *kind-hearted/sulky* – she'll do anything to help anyone.

2 Once when I was a child, my twin brother got better birthday presents than me. I was so *dependable/jealous*, and didn't speak to him for days!

3 My piano teacher is very *encouraging/mean*. She tells me I will be really good if I practise.

4 He's a very *upbeat/generous* person, and is always in a good mood.

5 After we had that argument, she became really *encouraging/sulky*, and didn't speak to me.

6 She said she forgot my birthday, but I think she's just too *kind-hearted/mean* to buy a present!

7 We are looking for a hardworking, *dependable/selfish* person to join our team of nurses at Free United Hospital.

8 My work colleague Paul is very *pleasant/jealous*, and always fun to be around.

**2** Choose the correct answer, a or b.

1 If someone is *sulky*, what does this mean?
 a They are in a bad mood, and might not speak to you.
 b They want to help people.

2 Someone who is *upbeat* is …
 a helpful and kind.
 b cheerful and positive about life.

3 Two words with opposite meanings are …
 a *generous* and *mean*.
 b *upbeat* and *dependable*.

4 Someone who thinks of themselves before they think of someone else is …
 a selfish.  b jealous.

5 A person who helps someone else to feel more confident is …
 a encouraging.  b dependable.

## Pronunciation | sounds and spelling: *ea*

**3** **a** Each sentence has four words with 'ea'. Three of them have the same sound, and one of them has a different sound. Circle the one with the different sound.

*She only buys cheap meat – she's (really) mean.*

1 The teacher was upbeat about her heart disease.

2 I'm fearful that it will take a year to clear this frozen meat.

3 I'm jealous, because each day you have a healthier breakfast than me.

4 My colleague realised she had ear problems when she was in the theatre.

5 I've read that the weather is very pleasant every season in the Canary Isles.

**b** 🔵 3 Listen and check.

**c** Complete the table with the 'ea' words in exercise 3a according to their sounds. Listen again and check.

| /iː/ | /e/ | /ɪə/ | /aː/ |
|---|---|---|---|
| cheap<br>meat<br>mean | | really | |

## How to... | start a conversation with a stranger

**4** Complete the conversation starters with a word from the box.

> are  couldn't  Do  do  Have  haven't

1 Hello, we _____ met, have we? I'm Anthony.

2 So _____ you enjoying the party?

3 _____ you tried these snacks?

4 Sorry, I _____ help overhearing. You said you've just been to Delhi?

5 _____ you know many people here?

6 So what _____ you think of this music?

**5** Match the conversation starters (1–6) in exercise 4 with the replies (a–f).

a To be honest, I think it's a bit too loud!

b Yes, I am. There's a great buffet, isn't there?

c No, I don't think we have. My name's Ivan.

d No, I haven't actually. But they look delicious – what are they?

e Not really. Just the hosts, and a couple of their friends. What about you?

f Yes, that's right. I was there on holiday. It's an amazing place. Have you been?

# Grammar | Present Simple and Present Continuous

**6** Find and correct the mistakes in four of the sentences.

1 I'm not understanding you – can you say it again, please?
2 Are you wanting to go home yet?
3 What do you mean?
4 He's having a very good job.
5 Excuse me, do you know the time?
6 They want to get married.
7 Do you have a large family?
8 I'm knowing a lot of people through Facebook.

**7** Complete the sentences with the Present Simple or Present Continuous form of the verbs in brackets.

1 **A:** How is your English?
 **B:** Not bad. It _____ (get) better.
2 I usually _____ (finish) work at six o'clock, and it _____ (take) me ten minutes to walk home.
3 You should turn your lights on. It _____ (get) dark.
4 _____ you always _____ (listen) to music in the car?
5 I _____ (live) with my parents until I can find an apartment to buy.
6 **A:** Shall we go out for a walk?
 **B:** Not now. It _____ (rain).

# Listening

**8** **a** ⊙ 4 Cover the audioscript. Listen to the psychologist. What is she talking about?

1 girlfriends and boyfriends
2 online relationships
3 work relationships

---

## AUDIOSCRIPT

The friends you have on a social networking site can help you enjoy your day at work, but don't expect too much from them as many of these 'online friends' prefer to stay online only.

My friend Patricia, met a friend of a friend, Howard, at a conference. They got on really well and started an online relationship. They found that they had a lot in common. They shared memories, and talked about their workmates. Sometimes they swapped more than twelve messages a day. Patricia looked forward to receiving Howard's messages when she arrived at work.

After a few weeks, however, Patricia asked Howard if he wanted to meet up after work, but he always found an excuse not to. Then she received a really strange message from him explaining how he didn't want to have a relationship and how he had decided to stop contacting her. That was the end of the story, and she never heard from him again.

You see, an online relationship takes a lot less energy than a face-to-face relationship. So a lot of people who don't really want the responsibility will try online friends instead. It's easier and, if you have an argument, you can always just shut down your computer!

---

**b** Listen again. Choose the correct answer, a or b.

1 Online friends are good for ...
 a going out with after work.
 b spending time with while you are at work.
2 Patricia and Howard ...
 a were old friends.  b met at a conference.
3 They talked about ...
 a their colleagues.  b their problems.
4 They usually sent ...
 a lots of messages every day.
 b one or two messages a day.
5 Patricia asked Howard to ...
 a meet her after work.  b stop contacting her.
6 Howard ...
 a wanted to go to the cinema with Patricia.
 b didn't want to meet her in person.
7 Online relationships use ...
 a more energy than face-to-face relationships.
 b less energy than face-to-face relationships.
8 The advantage of an online relationship is that if you argue, you can ...
 a switch off your computer.  b meet for a coffee.

## Vocabulary | arguing

**1**  **a**  Match the beginning of the phrases (1–7) with the end of the phrases (a–g).

1  get
2  see
3  fall
4  have an
5  not be in
6  not speak
7  lose your

a  red
b  argument
c  angry with someone
d  to someone for years
e  temper with someone
f  touch with someone any more
g  out with someone over money

**b**  Read the text. Who are the people in the photo?

José was my best friend at school. But one day we had argument about money. I remember I got really angry him. I said some horrible things to him. He lost temper and shouted at me. We completely out, and didn't speak to each other years after that. That was all many years ago now.

And now? Well, believe it or not, my son has just married José's daughter! And José and I are touch every day, just like before.

**c**  There are six words missing in the text. Add the words in the correct places.

## Grammar | Present Perfect Simple and Past Simple

**2**  Complete the text with the verbs from the box.

> finished    has lived    have always admired
> have been married    have just bought    have never been
> looked after    met    moved    spent

I (1) _____ my older brother – he's a really dependable person. He often (2) _____ me when I was little, because my parents were away a lot. Since he (3) _____ university, he (4) _____ in six different countries. He (5) _____ four years in Russia, where he (6) _____ a Russian lady called Tatiana. They (7) _____ for two years now. Last month he and Tatiana (8) _____ to Thailand. I (9) _____ there, but I've always wanted to go. And I'm really excited – I (10) _____ my plane ticket!

**3**  Complete the second sentence so that it means the same as the first. Use the verbs in brackets. Make sure you use the correct tense.

He became a lawyer in 2009.
He *has been a lawyer since* 2009. (be)

1  My parents keep dogs. They started when I was six years old.
   My parents _____ I was six years old. (keep)
2  Joan is in Paris. She went a week ago.
   Joan _____ a week. (be)
3  I met them two years ago.
   I _____ two years. (know)
4  She bought that car five years ago.
   She _____ five years. (have)
5  Alice moved to the countryside in 2010.
   Alice _____ 2010. (live).

**4**  Some sentences below have mistakes. Correct the mistakes and tick (✓) the correct sentences.

1  I haven't seen Maria for a couple of months.  ☐
2  I've had a headache since lunchtime.  ☐
3  I haven't had a cigarette since three weeks!  ☐
4  I've known Julia for we went to university.  ☐
5  I've lived here since ten years.  ☐
6  I have studied English since I was at school.  ☐
7  Have you been here since a long time?  ☐

**5**  Choose the correct word in *italics* to complete the sentences.

1  My daughter is just one year old, but she's *already/yet* learned to say 'hello'.
2  Oh no! I've *just/since* cut myself.
3  When I was a child I lived in China *already/for* a year.
4  Have you finished *yet/ago*?
5  We've been close friends *just/since* we were children.
6  My grandfather founded the firm fifty years *ago/for*.

## Vocabulary | phrasal verbs

**6** Complete the sentences with words from the box.

> after (x2)    brought    got    looked
> on    told    up

1   I was _____ up to enjoy music. My parents were very musical.
2   I take _____ my mother – she's a pianist, and so am I.
3   He was a professional musician, so I _____ up to him for that.
4   When I left home, I carried _____ playing.
5   I sometimes looked _____ his dog when he had a concert.
6   I _____ on well with Joey, the singer, who lived next door.
7   My mother always _____ me off for not practising the piano enough.
8   I grew _____ in New Orleans.

## Reading

**7** Read the article about the Radwanska sisters, then tick (✓) the correct summary, 1, 2 or 3.

1   The sisters often fall out because they are too competitive.
2   The sisters get on extremely well, even when they play against each other.
3   The sisters' relationship has got worse since they became professional.

**8** Read the article again. Mark the sentences true (T), false (F) or not given (NG).

1   The Radwanska sisters are now more famous around the world than the Williams sisters.
2   Agnieszka is older than Ula.
3   The girls' parents are closely involved in their tennis careers.
4   The Radwanska sisters have often played against the Williams sisters.
5   The girls make all their own travel arrangements.
6   The girls became professional players at the age of fifteen.
7   Agnieszka doesn't enjoy being famous.

# Sisterly love?

If you hear the words 'tennis' and 'sisters', you probably think of Venus and Serena Williams. But now we're hearing more and more about Poland's tennis superstars, the Radwanska sisters, Agnieszka and Ula.

Agnieszka has beaten some of the top players in the world, including Venus Williams and Martina Hingis. She has won professional competitions in Sweden, Thailand, Turkey and the UK.

Ula, her younger sister, is also a rising star. She was ranked as the world's number one junior player when she was sixteen.

Like the Williams sisters, the Radwanskas have their father as their coach. He is proud of his daughters' success, but says that it is only just beginning. He's brought the girls up to play tennis. And their mother helps them by dealing with their paperwork and booking flights.

During the tennis season, which lasts from January to October, the family travel round the world together. Wherever in the world they are, they try to rent a house together. They're obviously on the same wavelength. But does spending so much time together ever get a bit too much?

According to Ula, they get on really well, and hardly ever argue. Agnieszka is also very upbeat, and says that as they live together, they do everything together. They have been playing tennis together since they were in their teens, and there's only an age gap of one year between them. But whoever wins on the tennis court, they remain close.

For those few months when they're not playing tennis, they enjoy normal life back in Krakow. But they're big celebrities in Poland, and people really look up to them because of their success. So how do they deal with all the attention?

Ula says they often get recognised in taxis and so on. Agnieszka says that very often, when someone recognises them, they just look, but don't say anything. Perhaps they're too scared!

# Review and consolidation unit 1

## Auxiliary verbs (*do*, *be*, *have*)

**1** Write questions from the prompts.

1  you/live/in Thailand?

   _____

   Yes, I do.

2  you/see/the James Bond film/last night?

   _____

   No, we didn't.

3  When/Sal/go/on holiday?

   _____

   Next week.

4  What/sports/you/interested in?

   _____

   Tennis and basketball.

5  You/enjoy/study?

   _____

   Yes, I do.

6  You/forget/your books?

   _____

   Yes, I have.

7  Tim/like/working for IBM?

   _____

   Yes, he does.

8  You/happy/in/your new flat?

   _____

   Yes, I am.

9  George/have a good time/party yesterday?

   _____

   Yes, he did.

10 You/pass/all your exams?

   _____

   Yes, I have!

## Present tenses

**2** Choose the correct words in *italics*.

1  We *flying/fly/have flown* from Heathrow airport at 9:30 a.m.

2  What *are/have/do* you enjoy spending your money on?

3  Private schools *are/are being/have been* very expensive in China nowadays.

4  It *isn't seeming/hasn't seemed/doesn't seem* like a good idea to me.

5  Do you want to borrow this book? I *am just finishing/'ve just finished/just finish* it, and it was brilliant!

6  I'm afraid she's busy at the moment. She *talks/has talked/'s talking* to someone on the other line.

7  I *'m trying/have tried/is trying* to get fit, so I cycle to work every day.

8  I *'ve always enjoyed/'m always enjoying/'ve always enjoy* painting.

9  She works in the sales department, but I *can't remember/'m not remembering/haven't remembered* her name.

**3** Complete the dialogues with the verbs in brackets. Make sure you use the correct tense.

A: (1) _____ you ever _____ to San Francisco? (be)

B: Yes, I (2) _____ there a few years ago. (go)

A: (3) _____ you _____ it? (enjoy)

B: I (4) _____ it was fantastic! (think)

A: (5) _____ you _____ squash regularly? (play)

B: Yes. I (6) _____ quite good at it. (be)

A: How long (7) _____ you _____ for? (play)

B: I (8) _____ about six years ago. (start)

A: (9) _____ you _____ to play on Sunday? (want)

B: That (10) _____ like a great idea! (sound)

**4** Complete the sentences with *for* or *since*.

1  I haven't heard from him _____ ages.

2  We've been touring _____ last month.

3  They've been gone _____ yesterday.

4  Have you been waiting _____ long?

5  I've played the guitar _____ I was sixteen years old.

6  She's staying there _____ a few weeks.

7  We haven't seen Horace _____ he left home.

8  We lived in Spain _____ fifteen years.

9  He's been crying _____ this morning.

10 We've wanted to tell you _____ the weekend.

**5** There is a mistake in each sentence. Correct the mistakes.

1  We went to school together, so I've know her for a long time.

2  Have you spoke to the manager?

3  When have they got married?

4  We haven't been in touch since a long time.

5  When did you started working together?

6  I've never did see that programme.

7  It's the funniest book I've never read.

8  She have had a hair cut.

9  I've just start to learn Tai Kwando.

10 I haven't did sign the contract yet.

## Vocabulary

**6** Match the sentence beginnings (1–8) with the sentence endings (a–h).

1 My friend John is the life and soul
2 She fell out with her brother
3 I'm not very good
4 Sarah and I understand each other perfectly – we're really
5 I love bikes, so I belong
6 She's really kind – she would do anything
7 Ali's just started learning Russian, and he's already fluent
8 I'm not enjoying work – I don't get on well

a) for her friends.
b) in six languages!
c) on the same wavelength.
d) at tennis, but I'm having lessons.
e) over money, and they don't speak any more.
f) of the party – he's always making people laugh.
g) with my boss. But my other colleagues are nice.
h) to a cycling club, and we go out most weekends.

**7** Complete the text with the words in the box.

get   got  (x 2)   had  (x 4)

Some people think that a good friend is someone you never fall out with. I disagree. Let me tell you about one of my closest friends, Alberto.

I first (1) _____ to know him when we were at school. We were soon best friends. We (2) _____ the same sense of humour, and laughed at the same things. But when we were about ten, everything changed. Alberto and I (3) _____ an argument – I can't even remember what it was about now, but it made me see red at the time. We both (4) _____ angry. I didn't get in touch with him again.

About fifteen years later, I met a stranger on a train. We started talking, and I found we (5) _____ a lot in common. He (6) _____ an opinion about everything, and he was great fun to be around. I asked his name, and he said, 'Don't you remember? It's me, Alberto!' (He had a beard now, and I didn't recognise him.)

So now we're friends again. And I think we (7) _____ on even better now than when we were children!

**8** Put the letters in the correct order to make words to complete the sentences.

1 It was very _____ (slehsif) of you to take that last piece of cake!
2 I was often _____ (jeusola) when my brother got better Christmas presents than me.
3 Ali's really _____ (deapbnleed), and you can always go to him for help.
4 She's quite a _____ (eapstlna) lady, who's always happy to have a chat.
5 I can't stand _____ (name) people who never buy drinks for other people.
6 My driving instructor has been very _____ (eounigirncga), and helped me feel more confident.

**9** Choose the correct word in *italics*.

1 He *told/took/said* me off for being late.
2 The factory was taken *in/up/over* by a German business.
3 I have always looked *over/down/up to* my older brother.
4 My mother looks *up to/after/on* my baby son when I am at work.
5 He has used *over/up/by* all the paper.
6 We were brought *on/in/up* to eat everything on our plates, and never to waste food.
7 I *grew/belong/take* up in the countryside, but moved to the city when I got my first job.
8 I generally get *off/on/to* well with people at work.
9 I don't see him very often but we keep *in/off/on* touch by email.
10 I'm very organised. I take *on/off/after* my mother.

## How to...

**10** Put the words in the correct order to make questions.

1 always/crowded?/this/Is/it

_____

2 how/So,/do/you/Sara?/know

_____

3 these/Have/tried/sandwiches?/you

_____

4 time?/Excuse/tell/me/me,/could/you/the

_____

11

## Vocabulary | media

**1**  **a**  Choose the correct word in *italics* to complete the sentences.

1  Do you watch a lot of *real/reality* shows?
2  Do you do a lot of *immediate/instant* messaging?
3  Shall we watch the *horror/terror* film on TV tonight?
4  What did you think of the *thriller/thrilling* we saw last week?
5  Have you ever cried while you were watching a *romantic/romance* film?
6  Do you always look at the *contemporary/current* affairs section in your paper?

a  No, I hate them, but I love watching *soap/soaps*.
b  Sure, I do it most of the time when I'm *on/online*.
c  Not very often, I'm more interested in reading the *gossip/gossips*.
d  It was brilliant – I thought it was absolutely *unwatchable/gripping*.
e  Yes, I have once, but it was a really *moved/moving* story. What about you?
f  I don't like the sound of that. How about the *history/period* drama on the other channel?

**b**  Match the questions (1–6) with the answers (a–f) in exercise 1a.

## Vocabulary | film

**2**  Match the films (1–6) with the kinds of film in the box.

> animated film   docu-drama   horror film
> period drama   romantic comedy   thriller

**BIG SCREEN CINEMA – What's on this week**

1  *Escape from the Mob* – an exciting story of two lovers who are running away from dangerous gangsters.
2  *I Love You Stupid* – set in New York, this funny love story between a millionaire and shopkeeper will make you laugh until you cry!
3  *Barack Obama: the early years* – using real footage and actors playing the young Obama at different times in his life, this is a fascinating picture of the man who became President.
4  *Frogz* – a great new cartoon picture. Perfect for children – and adults as well!
5  *For the Love of a Prince* – this historical film, set in London in around 1800, has fabulous costumes and great acting.
6  *Dracula Returns* – he's dangerous, he's thirsty for blood, and he's back! The terrifying story of Count Dracula will make you scream!

## Grammar | defining relative clauses

**3**  Complete the sentences (1–6) with the correct phrases (a–f). Use *who/whose/which/where* to join the two phrases. You will need to omit some words.

1  That's the man _____
2  I like people _____
3  I've got an old car _____
4  Ella works in a factory _____
5  Laguna has a big beach _____
6  I spoke to the architect _____

a  it makes jewellery.
b  his wife won the lottery.
c  it never goes wrong.
d  you can surf there all year.
e  she is designing my house.
f  they are always honest.

**4**  **a**  Complete the sentences with *who*, *whose*, *which* or *where*.

1  Chicago was the place _____ Philippe Petit made his famous walk in 1974.
2  A documentary is a TV programme _____ gives factual information about a topic.
3  The journalist _____ made the film *Supersize Me* is called Michael Moore.
4  The translations _____ appear onscreen during a film are called 'subtitles'.
5  The address _____ the French President lives is Number 20, Champs-Élysées, Paris.
6  Russell Crowe is an actor from New Zealand _____ most famous film role was probably as the star of *Gladiator*.

**b**  Mark the sentences true (T) or false (F).

## How to... | give opinions and disagree

**5** Complete the dialogue with words from the box.

> do  on  opinion  reckon  sense  sure
> true  What

**A:** I (1) _____ everyone loves animated films. It doesn't matter how old you are. What's your (2) _____ ?

**B:** I'm not (3) _____ about that. I love them, but my mum hates them. Some people never watch cartoons.

**A:** That's (4) _____ , but I think most people like them. Children definitely do.

**B:** Yeah. I guess it depends (5) _____ the person, because everybody's different. (6) _____ do you think?

**A:** Yes, I think that makes (7) _____ .

**B:** So what's the best ever animated film? What (8) _____ you think?

**A:** That's difficult. There are so many ...

## Lifelong learning | using the media!

**6** Put the words in the correct order to make questions.

1 ever/message/you/your/instant/friends?/Do
2 often/you/How/do/go/cinema?/to/the
3 best/the/film/What's/ever/you/seen?/'ve
4 Do/know/been/anyone/you/TV?/who's/on
5 seen?/the/What's/funniest/'ve/comedy/you/ever
6 affairs?/the/way/to/What's/best/about/learn/current
7 Do/TV/prefer/watching/you/on/programmes/ online?/or

## Reading

**7** **a** Choose the best headline for the story, 1, 2 or 3.

1 Chilean newspaper celebrates its birthday
2 Chile paper lets readers choose the news
3 Chile's journalists stop writing serious news

**b** Read the article again and mark the sentences true (T) or false (F).

1 LUN was always a very successful newspaper. ☐
2 LUN uses Internet technology to find out which stories are popular. ☐
3 LUN's most popular articles are usually very serious stories. ☐
4 Augustine Edwards thinks LUN is popular because it has stories that people want to read. ☐
5 At the moment LUN pays more money to the journalists if they write popular stories. ☐
6 The article suggests at least half of Chileans don't read www.lun.com. ☐

## A newspaper with a difference

**It was over 100 years old, boring and unpopular. But now Las Ultimas Noticias (LUN: The Latest News), has become one of Chile's favourite newspapers. Employees at LUN say it's a revolution in journalism. Critics say it's rubbish.**

Recently LUN started analysing their web traffic statistics on www.lun.com. The clicks tell the editors which stories are popular and which are not. If an article gets a lot of clicks, the newspaper continues the story the following day, or finds similar ones. If an article gets only a few clicks, the story is killed. According to Augustine Edwards, the newspaper's publisher, LUN reflects the changing values and interests of Chile.

So, what news did readers choose when world leaders arrived in Santiago for an important trade meeting? One of the top stories was about where the US Secretary of State went to dinner and what he ate (prawns with couscous). Another popular story was about which politicians gave the best tips to the waiters (the Japanese).

The critics say LUN now has no serious news. Edwards replies, 'I'm focused not on what people should read, but what they want to read. I want my journalists to write for the people, not for me or their editors.' He even plans to pay his journalists according to the number of clicks their stories get.

However, only the richest half of the country has Internet access. So one question remains: is LUN really a reflection of 'the changing values and interests of Chile'?

## Vocabulary | television

**1** Match the sentence beginnings (1–6) with the sentence endings (a–f).

1  I need to get a new TV
2  Is there anything good on
3  They say that if you work on live
4  My cousin has a new job as a TV
5  I'm so happy we've now got digital
6  I'm a football fan, so my favourite TV

a  TV tonight?
b  channel is Eurosport.
c  producer for Al Jazeera.
d  set because my old one is broken.
e  TV, you shouldn't work with animals or children!
f  TV, because we have lots more channels than before.

## Pronunciation |
/n/ and /ŋ/

**2  a** Read the text and <u>underline</u> all the /ŋ/ sounds. How many /ŋ/ sounds can you find?

> I started chatting to someone on the bus home from college yesterday. This woman – she said her name was Angela – told me that I just had to watch a film on TV that evening. She said it was the most entertaining film she'd ever seen. So when I got home, I switched on the TV to watch it.
>
> It was about bank robbers. They went into banks and started singing, so all the people just laughed at them. They didn't know they were dangerous criminals. The film wasn't a comedy – it certainly wasn't very funny. But it wasn't a thriller either. It was more boring than exciting. In fact, I turned it off after a few minutes, because it was just unwatchable. It just goes to show – never listen to what you're told by a stranger on a bus!

**b** 🔊 5 Now listen and check.

## Grammar | the passive

**3** Complete the second sentence with no more than three words so that it means the same as the first sentence.

Mr Turner founded CNN in 1980.

CNN _was founded by_ Mr Turner in 1980.

1  The editor doesn't write many articles.
   Not many articles _____ the editor.
2  Japanese workers made the TV set.
   The TV set _____ Japanese workers.
3  A group of large banks are organising the meeting.
   The meeting _____ a group of large banks.
4  The player has signed the contract today.
   The player's contract _____ today.
5  The media will cover any scandal.
   Any scandal _____ by the media.
6  You can find branches of our company in most countries in the world.
   Branches of our company can _____ in most countries.
7  Australians buy 2.5 million newspapers each day.
   2.5 million newspapers _____ each day.
8  *Avatar* sold over $1 billion dollars' worth of tickets in its first seventeen days.
   Over $1 billion dollars' worth of *Avatar* cinema tickets _____ in its first seventeen days.

## How to... | describe an object

**4** Complete each sentence with one word.

1  It's used _____ changing channels on the TV.
2  It's circular, made _____ metal, and you can buy things with it.
3  It's an adjective, and its meaning is similar _____ 'annoying'.
4  These are used _____ people who have an mp3 player.
5  It looks _____ a mobile, but you can't make calls with it.
6  It's a kind _____ computer.

**5** Match the items in the box with the descriptions (1–6) in exercise 4.

> a calculator    a coin    a notebook    a TV remote control
> headphones    the word *nauseating*

# When no news is real news – the journalists who lied and got caught

Open a newspaper and you expect to read, more or less, the truth. So what happens when it turns out that journalists invent their stories? Ask Janet Cooke or Stephen Glass or Ingo Mocek. They all spent parts of their careers inventing stories before being caught and **fired**.

Imagine the scene: Washington DC, 1980. Janet Cooke writes a long article for *The Washington Post* describing the world of eight-year-old Jimmy, a child living in terrible conditions in the poorest part of the city.

She writes about every detail of his life, even describing the 'baby-smooth skin of his thin brown arms'. The story shocks Washington, and Cooke wins a Pulitzer Prize for outstanding journalism. But when the city government tries to find Jimmy to help him, Cooke goes quiet.
**Under pressure**, she eventually admits that Jimmy doesn't exist.

Stephen Glass, a **star reporter** at *The New Republic* magazine, invented stories for years. 'My life was one very long process of lying and lying again to work out how to cover those other lies,' he says. Glass made great efforts to avoid getting caught. He created fake notes, fake faxes, fake email

addresses; he even designed a website for a company that didn't exist. Eventually, he got caught when he wrote a story about a fifteen-year-old boy at a conference of computer **hackers**. His editor **insisted** on seeing the conference room. Of course, there was no conference room. And no conference either. And no fifteen-year-old boy. Glass's career as a journalist was finished, but he wrote a novel about his life, *The Fabulist*.

And sometimes **celebrities** and their fans are involved too. In 2010, the German magazine *Neon*, published an interview with Beyoncé. The article contained a lot of information about the star and her marriage to rapper Jay-Z which Beyoncé's fans thought might not be true. The editors questioned the journalist, Ingo Mocek, about the article she had written. It turned out that she had invented much of the information – in fact, the interview probably never took place at all. Ingo Mocek was **fired**, and *Neon* made an apology to Beyoncé and her management.

The message for us, the public? Don't believe everything you read, even if it comes from your favourite, trusted newspaper!

## Reading

**6** **a** Read the article and choose the best endings (a, b or c) for the sentences.

1  Janet Cooke was
   a  a very poor woman.
   b  a journalist.
   c  a newspaper editor.

2  She invented a story about
   a  a child living a difficult life.
   b  a man called Jimmy.
   c  the government.

3  The city government
   a  fired Cooke.
   b  tried to find the boy.
   c  didn't believe the story.

4  Stephen Glass created
   a  a magazine.
   b  a false identity for himself.
   c  fake papers to pretend he was telling the truth.

5  Stephen Glass was caught
   a  quickly.
   b  by the police.
   c  after many years.

6  When Beyoncé's fans read the article, they
   a  thought it was well-written.
   b  did not believe it.
   c  were angry with Beyoncé.

7  Ingo Mocek lost her job because she had
   a  been rude to Beyoncé during the interview.
   b  interviewed Beyoncé without permission.
   c  not interviewed Beyoncé at all.

**b** Find the words or expressions in **bold** in the article that mean …

1  people who break into technological systems illegally _____
2  top journalist _____
3  removed from a job _____
4  demanded _____
5  in a stressful situation _____
6  famous people (e.g. pop stars) _____

# Pronunciation | word stress on word endings

**1** **a** Look at the words in *italics* in the sentences. Is the stress the same or different?

I learnt some *Portuguese* when I was in *Portugal*. PORtugal PortuGUESE (different)

1 '*Escaping* was easy,' said the *escapee*.
2 Both *employers* and *employees* are happy with the deal.
3 Lots of *Burmese* and *Chinese* people live in the region.
4 No *divorcee* actually enjoys *divorcing*.
5 Being a *carer* is a very rewarding *career*.

**b**  6 Now listen and check.

# Grammar | Past Simple and Past Continuous

**2** Complete the newspaper articles with the Past Simple or Past Continuous form of the verbs in brackets.

## Young boy, 5, discovered 300 kilometres from home

Police who (1) _____ (look) for a lost five-year-old boy eventually (2) _____ (find) him the next day. After getting separated from his family in a market, the boy, from Pekanbaru in Malaysia, (3) _____ (go) to a station, got onto a train, and was discovered in Padang, 300 kilometres away. 'He (4) _____ (be) very calm,' said the boy's mother. 'It was us, his family, who (5) _____ (worry) all night.'

## Traffic jams make Angelenos feel at home

A recent study said that Los Angeles has the worst traffic in the United States. Last year Angelenos (6) _____ (spend) an average of 136 hours a year stuck in traffic. Only last week a man was arrested while he (7) _____ (brush) his teeth in the car, and drivers are regularly seen applying make-up and shaving. Police (8) _____ (say) that yesterday they (9) _____ (stop) a man who (10) _____ (drive) while playing on his laptop computer.

**3** Look at the pictures and complete the sentences with the Past Simple or Past Continuous form of the verbs in brackets.

1 Someone _____ (steal) my wallet while I _____ (not/look).

2 I _____ (not/know) you _____ (be) in town.

3 We _____ (not/hear) the burglar because we _____ (listen) to loud music.

4 I _____ (drive) home when I _____ (see) a black cat at the side of the road.

5 Eve _____ (not/take) the bus because it _____ (be) a beautiful day.

6 Josie _____ (meet) Clyde while they _____ (ski).

## Vocabulary | in the news

**4** **a** Match the sentence beginnings (1–5) with the endings (a–e).

1 Someone told me that the President has broken
2 Congratulations – I hear you're having
3 Spain won the
4 A lot of accidents
5 I hear most banks have made

a match 2 – 1.
b a baby – when is it due?
c up with his wife – is it true?
d huge profits again this year.
e are caused by drivers on mobile phones.

**b** Match the replies (a–e) with the sentences (1–5) in exercise 4a.

a I know – why can't people be more responsible?
b Yes, they played brilliantly.
c Yes, I know, I've just been reading about it in the business section.
d Thank you, it's next month, and we think it's a girl.
e Oh come on, you can't believe all the gossip you hear!

## Listening

**5** **a** 7 Cover the audioscript. Listen to the local news headlines and complete the notes.

1 Children eat too much _____ , says nutritionist.
2 1,000 _____ to be destroyed.
3 _____ saves car crash victims.
4 Artist sells painting to _____ .

> **AUDIOSCRIPT**
>
> And now for today's news headlines.
> A nutritionist says our children are eating too much fat.
> In Fincher, one thousand homes will be destroyed to build a shopping area.
> A taxi driver last night saved two lives after a car crash.
> And local artist Angela Witco sells a painting to rock star, Lee Santana.

**b** 8 Cover the audioscript. Listen to the news stories and answer the questions.

1 Who did Niall Smith study?
2 What food and drink should the children eat and drink less of?
3 What two things will the town of Fincher build in place of the houses?
4 When will the new houses be built?
5 Who did John Manley save?
6 Where exactly did he take them?
7 Where did Lee Santana see the painting?
8 How does Witco feel about selling her painting to Lee Santana?

> **AUDIOSCRIPT**
>
> Nutritionist Niall Smith from the Cambridge Think Tank on Diet and Health, says that our children eat too much fatty food. In a two-year study of 900 schoolchildren aged eleven to fifteen, Smith and his team found that children eat double the amount of fat recommended by nutritionists. Hamburgers, chips, chocolate and fizzy soft drinks were the biggest problems.
>
> In the town of Fincher, one thousand homes will be knocked down to build a shopping area and car park. Local councillors say that the shopping area will revitalise Fincher town centre. They say new housing will be built next year.
>
> A taxi driver, John Manley, has saved the lives of a husband and wife whose car crashed into a tree on Friday night. Manley pulled the couple from the car and drove them immediately to a London hospital in his taxi. They are now in a stable condition.
>
> Painter Angela Witco has found a famous buyer for her work. Rock star and art lover Lee Santana bought Witco's painting *Trees in Winter* for an undisclosed sum. He saw the painting in a small art gallery in Manchester and fell in love with it immediately. Witco says she is extremely happy that her painting has found a good home.

# Review and consolidation unit 2

## Defining relative clauses

**1** Join the sentence pairs to make single sentences with *who/which/where/whose*. Make any necessary changes.

*The Vatican City is a state. The Pope lives there.*
*The Vatican City is the state where the Pope lives.*

1 Los Angeles is a city. Michael Jackson died there.

_____

2 Franz Kafka was a writer. He wrote a story about a man who became an insect.

_____

3 St Petersburg is a city. It used to be called Leningrad.

_____

4 Rodin was a sculptor. He made *The Thinker*.

_____

5 *Avatar* is a famous film. It cost $500,000,000 to make.

_____

6 Malibu is a beach in California. Hundreds of celebrities live there.

_____

7 Vivaldi was a composer. His most famous work was *The Four Seasons*.

_____

8 Istanbul is a city. It is built on two continents – Europe and Asia.

_____

**2** Complete the sentences using the prompts and the passive so that they mean the same as the first sentences. Use three or four words including the words in brackets.

*You can see the Great Wall of China from space!*
*The Great Wall of China is a structure which can be seen from space. (seen)*

1 That's the boy! Someone gave him my bicycle.
That's the boy _____ my bicycle! (was)

2 These are great stories. People tell them from generation to generation.
These are the great stories _____ from generation to generation. (told)

3 He's an artist. People buy his paintings for thousands of Euros.
He's the artist _____ for thousands of Euros. (sold)

4 That's the old country house. I was born there.
That's the old country house _____ . (was)

5 It's a type of pen. You can use it under water.
It's a type of pen _____ under water. (be)

6 These are the tourists. Someone has stolen their bags.
These are the tourists _____ stolen. (been)

## The passive, Past Simple and Past Continuous

**3** **a** Match the sentences beginnings (1–8) with the sentence endings (a–h).

1 Robin Kruger wasn't caught while he was

2 In his left hand he was carrying a small gun and ☐

3 A few hours later, he was captured at his home, ☐

4 He gave a note to Melanie Joseph, who ☐

5 Kruger was wearing sunglasses and a hat ☐

6 The note said 'I have a gun in my hand. ☐

7 Miss Joseph took the note and gave ☐

8 Police officer Don Callow explained, 'Kruger's note was 8

a was working at the bank as a cashier.
b where he was counting his money.
c Give me £10,000 in cash.'
d trying to rob a bank, but very soon afterwards.
e written on the back of an envelope with his address on it.'
f in his right hand he had a bag for the money.
g him the money, and he walked out.
h when he walked into the bank.

**b** Now put the sentences in the correct order to make the story. The first and the last sentences have been done.

**c** <u>Underline</u> five examples of the Past Continuous and (circle) three examples of the passive in the story in exercise 3a.

**4** Complete the sentences with the verbs in brackets in the correct form.

1 Last year, over $4,000,000,000 _____ (spend) on computers.

2 I hurt my back while I _____ (work) in the garden.

3 When _____ (you/realise) you had this great talent for tennis?

4 The car _____ (stop) by the police at 6:10 a.m. They searched it immediately.

5 I _____ (not/go) to the party because I had too much work to do.

6 Penicillin _____ (discover) by accident.

7 Who _____ (talk) to when I saw you this morning? I've never seen her before.

8 They didn't hear the news because they _____ (stay) on a desert island at that time.

# Vocabulary

**5** Complete the sentences with the words from the box.

> affairs   animated   chat   screen   sections

Welcome to Mediareview.com, the webpage for busy people! Mediareview.com tells you what's been in the newspapers and on TV this week.

It's been a great week for sports fans. The sports (1) _____ of all the newspapers have had all the matches from the International Open tennis men's finals. And I have to tell you I did enjoy watching the final on my big new flat (2) _____ TV – absolutely gripping! And there was a very entertaining interview with the champion on my favourite (3) _____ show, *Tonight with Jo King*.

But it's been a busy week if you're interested in current (4) _____ too, with all the pre-election news. And for film fans: the new Disney adventure, *Elephants in Space*, an (5) _____ film, is sure to be popular with the kids.

**6 a** Complete the table with the words and phrases in the box.

> athlete   cable   critic   digibox   film director
> lobster   monkey   reality show   seagull
> sitcom   soap   thriller

| things to watch | |
|---|---|
| animals | |
| equipment | |
| people | |

**b** Complete the sentences with the words and phrases in exercise 8a.

1 I watch this _____ every week. I want to know who's going to win.
2 Have you got a _____ to connect my camera to the computer?
3 She's a well-known _____ , and her movies have won prizes all over the world.
4 The _____ is the noisiest bird I know!
5 Plug the _____ into the back of your TV.
6 My brother is a theatre _____ , and sees five or six new plays every week.
7 The word '_____' comes from the words 'situation comedy'.
8 If you're a professional _____ , you need to train for several hours every day.
9 A TV _____ needs to sound, and look, brilliant all the time.
10 The only good thing about this _____ is the costumes. Apart from that, it's unwatchable rubbish!
11 Last time I watched a _____ , I was so terrified that I couldn't sleep afterwards.

# How to...

**7 a** Complete the sentences by adding one word.

1 reckon we should buy the black sofa, not the blue one.
2 What you think of that new Keira Knightley film?
3 You said we should leave at 8:00, but I'm not sure that.
4 I'd love to go to the beach, but it depends the weather.
5 If your computer isn't working, try turning off and on again.
6 What's matter with your TV? The picture isn't very good, is it?
7 If the microwave breaks down again, call us and we can fix immediately.

**b** Match the sentences (1–7) in exercise 7a with the responses (a–g).

a Me too. I think it'll be sunny.
b It depends on the traffic, but I think 8:15 will be OK.
c Great. I'll keep your phone number then.
d It depends how expensive the black one is.
e No, it isn't working properly. I can only get two channels.
f OK, I'll try that.
g I think it's brilliant. I loved the opening scene.

# 3 Lifestyle

## Vocabulary | lifestyle/home

**1  a**  Match the definitions (1–7) with the words and phrases in the box.

> attic  cellar  drive  outskirts  playground
> public transport  studio flat

1  parts of a town that are not close to the centre
2  private road or parking space between the street and a building
3  room or space (often with no windows) under a building
4  buses, trams, trains etc
5  room or space just below the roof of a house
6  one-room flat
7  an outdoor area for children to enjoy themselves, especially in a park

**b**  Complete the sentences with the words and phrases in the box in exercise 1a.

1  I often take my kids to the local _____ , where they play with their friends.
2  I live in a tiny _____ , but I'm looking for a bigger place.
3  I live on the _____ of the city, quite close to the countryside. It's 20 minutes by bus to the centre.
4  I've put all the old furniture (which I don't need) up in the _____ .
5  We keep the wine in the _____ because it is very cool down there.
6  My flat is great for _____ : the station's five minutes away, and the bus stops in front of my house.
7  You can park the car outside the house, on the _____ .

## Grammar | future plans

**2**  Complete the sentences with the *will* or *going to* form of the verbs in brackets.

1  A: Why are you reading all those books?
   B: _____ an English course in September. (I/start)
2  A: What would you like to drink?
   B: _____ some mineral water, please. (I/have)
3  A: I don't know how to work this computer programme.
   B: Don't worry. _____ you. (I/show)
4  A: Have you decided where to go on your birthday?
   B: Yes, it's all planned. _____ that new restaurant I told you about. (We/try)

**3**  Add one word to complete each sentence.

1  I need some fresh air. I think I go for a walk.
2  you seeing Jack at the weekend?
3  What time Susannah coming?
4  We going to Berlin at the end of the month.
5  Are you coming to the concert too? Great – we see you there then.

## How to... | complain politely

**4  a**  Complete the sentences with the words in the box.

> about  apologise  isn't  to (x2)  you

1  I don't like _____ complain, but these chips are cold.
2  You're an hour late! I think _____ should get here on time next time.
3  I still haven't received your payment. I'm sorry, but it just _____ good enough.

a  I do _____ for that. You'll have the money by tomorrow.
b  Oh, I'm sorry _____ hear that. I'll bring you some hot ones.
c  Yes, I know, I must apologise _____ that. I was stuck in traffic.

**b**  Match the sentences (1–3) with the sentences (a–c) in exercise 4a to make dialogues.

# Reading

**5** **a** Read the article and complete the table.

| | Jean-Marc, Felicity and Abrielle | Pat, John and Sally |
|---|---|---|
| Where is their house? | | |
| How many bedrooms are there? | | |
| Other features of the house/area | | |
| How much money does the hotel/bed and breakfast make per year? | | |
| How do they spend their time? | | |
| What do they want to get from the house swap? | | |

**b** What is different about this house swap?

## HOUSE SWAP WITH A DIFFERENCE

Swapping your house with another family is one thing. But would you be happy to swap not just your house, but also your business? This is exactly what the following two families decided to do.

Jean-Marc, Felicity and Abrielle (sixteen) live in a huge villa in the south of France. The house has six guest bedrooms, a swimming pool, vineyards and extensive gardens. They run a hotel from the house, earning more than €50,000 per year. They employ two full-time staff so that they can take time off work to swim, eat good food, play golf and generally enjoy the Mediterranean lifestyle.

They decided to swap lives with John, Pat and Sally for one month. They hoped that the swap would be useful work experience for their daughter Abrielle.

John, Pat and their daughter Sally live in Bongor, a seaside town in the north of England, famous for its fish and chips. They run a bed and breakfast, which has ten bedrooms, and earns €20,000 in the high season, and about €10,000 during the rest of the year. They work hard. John manages the finances and serves food and drinks to the guests. Sally works as a waitress and helps Pat in the kitchen. Pat does the shopping, cooking, cleaning the bedrooms, and anything else that needs to be done. Pat is exhausted and wants to spend a month in France, to see how different life could be.

We spoke to the couples after their swap to ask them how it went.

# Listening

**6** **a** 🔘 9 Cover the audioscript. Listen to Pat and Jean-Marc describing the house swap.

1 Was the swap a success for Pat?
2 Was the swap a success for Jean-Marc?

**b** Listen again and answer the questions about Pat.

1 Why was the house swap like a honeymoon?
2 What job did she have to do in the mornings?
3 What did they do with their free time?

**c** Now answer the questions about Jean-Marc.

1 Where did the English family live when they were at home?
2 Why didn't Jean-Marc like the traditional English breakfast?
3 Was the trip a success for Abrielle?
4 Would they like to repeat the experience?

---

**AUDIOSCRIPT**

**Pat:** It was wonderful. It was probably the best thing I've ever done. When we arrived at this beautiful villa it was like being on honeymoon. There was hardly any work to do. There was a cleaner for the rooms, and the only cooking I had to do was to make coffee in the morning! We had lots of free time, so we travelled around the area and went sailing. It didn't feel like work at all – it was a wonderful holiday.

**Jean-Marc:** Well, we were very surprised to see how the English family lived. They had two very small rooms in the basement, underground, and all the nice bedrooms were used for the guests. Also I think they work too hard, because nobody helps them. They are always cooking and cleaning. I had to cook a traditional English breakfast, but it was terrible. I can't eat food like that because I think it is very bad for you. In France we have fresh bread, with jam and coffee. It is healthier, and easier to prepare too! It was an interesting experience, but I was very happy to come home, and I don't think Abrielle learnt anything very useful. We wouldn't do it again.

# Vocabulary | adjectives for describing places

**1** **a** Match the adjectives (1–8) with their definitions (a–h) to make complete sentences.

| | | | |
|---|---|---|---|
| 1 | tiny | a | busy and full of people and traffic |
| 2 | dull | b | popular with visitors |
| 3 | touristy | c | dirty and unhealthy because of carbon emissions |
| 4 | bustling | | |
| 5 | polluted | d | boring |
| 6 | enormous | e | attractive |
| 7 | picturesque | f | very large |
| 8 | unwelcoming | g | unfriendly |
| | | h | very small |

**b** Complete the sentences with the adjectives (1–8) from exercise 1a.

a It's an absolutely _____ city, with over 20 million residents.

b My home town is so _____ . There's nothing to do, and nowhere to go.

c Hassop is a _____ village – it's only got three houses and a postbox!

d From the top of the hill, the town looks very _____ , so remember to take your camera.

e Big cities are often very _____ , and it's hard to meet people when you move there.

f When you go to Kengtung, you must visit the _____ market, which is full even at 6 o'clock in the morning.

g Seatown is pretty, but very very _____ . The town is full of coaches and people taking photographs and buying ice creams.

h Unfortunately, Sinston is badly _____ because of all the factories in the area.

# Grammar | comparatives and superlatives

**2** Complete the sentences with the comparative form of the adjectives in the box.

> expensive   heavy   modern   near   peaceful   small

1 It's very noisy in here. Shall we go somewhere _____ ?

2 The meal was cheap. I expected it to be _____ .

3 Your suitcase feels light. Mine is much _____ .

4 The style is a bit old-fashioned. I was looking for something _____ .

5 That hotel is a long way from the centre. Can't you find anything _____ ?

6 This table is enormous. Have you got anything _____ ?

**3** Complete the sentences with the comparative or superlative form of the adjectives in brackets.

1 They say London is the most interesting city in the world to visit. But I don't think it's the _____ place to live. (good)

2 Going out to eat in Milan was _____ than we expected. (expensive)

3 Delhi is the _____ city I have ever been to. (hot)

4 Madrid is a big, bustling city. The atmosphere in Salamanca is _____ . (relaxed)

5 Ravenna has some of the _____ mosaics in the world. (beautiful)

6 Istanbul is one of the _____ cities I know. (lively)

# Reading

**4** Read the information about a new book. Tick (✓) the statements which are correct.

The book …

1 provides information about different cities in the US. ☐

2 is a fictional description of life in New York. ☐

3 tells you which are the best and the worst cities to live in. ☐

4 describes twelve of the best European cities. ☐

5 might be useful for someone who is planning to move to the US. ☐

## Think your city is best?

### See the latest rankings.

The latest issue of *Cities Ranked and Rated* is just out. This book describes the top cities in the US. But what is it that makes a metropolis great (or bad)?

Are you thinking about relocating, or just curious how your city compares with others across the nation? Well, the answers to your questions are here, as featured in the annually updated book *Cities Ranked and Rated*. The book's authors, Bert Sterling and Peter Sander, talked to us about their findings.

**5** Read the article below and match the questions (1–6) with the answers (a–f).

1 If I'm young and single, just starting out, what places would I find attractive?

2 And what if I have a family with kids? Is that different?

3 In general, what places make it to the top of the list?

4 How did you decide who makes it to the top?

5 Were there any surprises in your findings?

6 And what about the bad news? Why does a city end up at the bottom of your list?

a We look at over a hundred pieces of information about each place. We group those into nine categories including: economy and jobs, cost of living, climate, education, arts and culture. Then we press a button on the computer, and that's how we get the top ten.

b Cities with a university do especially well. They have plenty to do, nice city centres, pleasant surroundings and usually they aren't too crowded. The strength in higher education tends to affect all levels of education and most have excellent health care facilities. Then there are the state capitals, which tend to be clean, have a good economic situation and lots of cultural facilities – these are also good.

c Yes, quite a few. For instance, highly ranked cities are found all across the country, not just on the sunny coastlines like everybody thinks. There are a few interesting cities that we call the 'Big City Bargains'. These are big cities with a low cost of living, like Pittsburgh and Indianapolis.

d Areas at the bottom typically have high levels of unemployment and crime and a high cost of living combined with low levels of education, few facilities and not much to do. However, most of these cities recognise that there are problems and they are actively working to improve.

e Younger single people are interested in places with jobs where they can build their careers and make money. They want lively cities with lots to do, and of course lots of other single people too! Of course, the top ten cities would all be good places to live, but for singles in particular we would choose the Norfolk area in Virginia and San Antonio, Texas.

f Yes. Families look for many things, including good and affordable housing, quality education and more daytime facilities like parks, museums and outdoor recreation.

**6** Choose the best answers, a, b or c.

1 The authors decided on the top cities by …
   a asking people about their favourite cities.
   b looking at the population of each city.
   c comparing statistics about each city.

2 According to the book, university cities …
   a have a lot of crime.
   b are nice cities to live in.
   c usually have too many people.

3 Cities with lots of people in higher education also tend to …
   a have a low cost of living.
   b have good hospitals and doctors.
   c come near the bottom of the list.

4 The top cities …
   a are found on the coasts.
   b are cheap to live in.
   c are spread across the country.

5 'Big City Bargains' are cities which …
   a are cheap to live in.
   b are expensive to live in.
   c have a low standard of living.

6 Cities at the bottom of the list …
   a don't realise that there is a problem.
   b have a lot of people who do not work.
   c are cheap to live in.

7 Young single people look for cities …
   a where they can get good jobs.
   b where there are a lot of parks and museums.
   c which are cheap to live in.

## Grammar | future possibility

**1** Put the words in the correct order to make sentences.

1 at/probably/party./you/'ll/the/see/We
2 not/He/want/might/come./to
3 airport/us/may/They/at/meet/the.
4 call/Simmons/the/Mrs/about/contract/might.
5 for/you/table/eight/book/please?/o'clock,/Could/a
6 you/buy/Do/house?/think/you/the/might/
7 to/won't/I/definitely/go/restaurant/that/again.
8 this/We/win/definitely/game./will

## Vocabulary | compound nouns

**2 a** Match the compound nouns in the box with the definitions (1–8).

air conditioning     bunk bed
central heating     fish tank
household waste     sofa bed     solar panels
washing machine

1 rubbish
2 for pets to swim in
3 something for cleaning clothes
4 these get energy from the sun
5 a system to keep your home warm
6 a system for keeping a building cool
7 a bed for two people, especially children
8 a piece of furniture that can be a seat or a bed

**b** Complete the sentences with the compound nouns from the box in exercise 2a.

1 It's hot. Shall I put the _____ on?
2 My flat is very cold because the _____ isn't working.
3 Can you put all the dirty clothes in the _____ please?
4 I'm going to put _____ on my roof, to make my own electricity.
5 I bought a cheap _____ online. So now I need some goldfish to put in it.
6 My brother and I shared a small bedroom, and slept in a _____. I had the top one.
7 The council collect _____ on Wednesdays, but only if we leave it outside in a black sack.
8 We have a _____ in the living room. It's great – guests sleep on it, as we don't have a spare bedroom.

## Pronunciation | word stress in compound nouns

**3 a** Look at the compound nouns in box A, and tick (✓) the correct sentence, a or b.

**A**

birdsong     computer screen     DVD player     fireplace
nightlife     skylight     swimming pool

a The compounds in box A consist of: [ADJECTIVE + NOUN]. ☐
b The compounds in box A consist of: [NOUN + NOUN]. ☐

**b** 🔘 10 Listen and mark the stress on the compounds in box A.

**c** Now look at the compound nouns in box B, and tick (✓) the correct sentence, a or b.

**B**

central heating     household waste     mobile phone
public transport     terraced house

a The compounds in box B consist of: [ADJECTIVE + NOUN]. ☐
b The compounds in box B consist of: [NOUN + NOUN]. ☐

**d** 🔘 11 Listen and mark the stress on the compounds in box B.

## Vocabulary | prefixes and suffixes

**4** Complete the words in the dialogues with prefixes and suffixes.

1 A: Is the coast full of hotels and bars?
   B: Not at all, it's totally _____spoilt.
2 A: I haven't seen your girlfriend for a long time. How is she?
   B: I don't know. She's my _____-girlfriend now.
3 A: I'm afraid I can't make the meeting tomorrow.
   B: That's not a problem. We can _____arrange it.
4 A: Do you get on with your new flat-mate?
   B: He's OK, but he's very mess_____ .
5 A: I paid over £5,000 for the insurance.
   B: That's unbeliev_____ !
6 A: I love it here. It's so quiet.
   B: Yes. It's very peace_____.
7 A: Where is Saskia?
   B: I don't know. It's _____usual for her to be late.
8 A: This is a table for six people, but we booked for twelve.
   B: I think there's been a _____understanding.

# Reading

**5** **a** Read the article and match the paragraph headings (a–d) with the paragraphs (1–4).

    a   The 'smart' home of the future
    b   Things your clothes might be able to do
    c   Predictions that were wrong
    d   Changes in information technology

**1** _____

People have always been interested in how things will change in the future. But we should remember that people have often got things wrong. I'll just give you two examples. In 1943, Thomas Watson, the founder of IBM (who make computers) was asked what he thought about the future of technology. And he said that one day there might be a worldwide market 'for maybe five computers'. Just five computers – can you imagine that?! And H.G. Wells, the writer, said that one day **public transport** would be moving walkways, like moving pavements, and you'd just step on and off to go anywhere you wanted.

**2** _____

Well, of course now we know that these predictions weren't **accurate**. But we can be fairly sure that developments in IT today will become the changes in our lifestyles tomorrow. And a lot of that will involve microchips. It's possible that by 2025, anything small enough to contain a microchip will have one.

**3** _____

So, for example, **household** technology might be very different. We could have fridges that can read the **use-by date** on your milk, and then place an order for more when you need it. Or our washing machines could be so smart that when something goes wrong, they send a message to a service engineer about the problem.

**4** _____

And even the things you wear could be connected to this technology. For example, a device could change your mobile to different **settings**, depending on whether you're in your work or casual clothes. No more annoying work calls when you're in the pub! And no more embarrassing football text messages when you're in a meeting!

But if you don't like the sound of all this, don't worry. Even H.G. Wells got the future wrong!

**b** Read the article again. Mark the sentences true (T) or false (F).

1 Thomas Watson thought that in the future, everyone would have a computer.
2 More things will have microchips in them.
3 Fridges will order your milk.
4 People will probably wear the same clothes at work and when they go out.

**c** Complete the sentences with the words and phrases in **bold** from the article.

1 I need to change the _____ on my mobile, because it's too quiet.
2 Where can I buy _____ objects – kettles, radios, an iron, that sort of thing?
3 My GPS isn't very _____ , so I often get lost on the road.
4 Check the _____ on that cheese – it's been in the fridge for ages!
5 Lisbon has great _____ , and it's so easy to get around.

# Review and consolidation unit 3

## Future plans

**1** Correct the mistakes in the following sentences.

1 We going to Mexico on holiday this year.
2 I don't think I go to the cinema tonight because I'm too tired.
3 Who is meet us at the airport?
4 We getting married in June.
5 Excuse me, I'll to have a cappuccino please.
6 We're going see Andrea tomorrow. Do you want to come with us?
7 A: I'm really hungry.
  B: OK. I go to make us some lunch now.
8 A: What are you doing at the weekend?
  B: We will go to visit my mother-in-law.
9 Do you will come with us to the office?
10 Can you tell Jonathan I see him later?
11 Do you coming to Madrid to watch the football?
12 Sue is leave for Brazil and I'm not going to see her any more.

## comparatives/superlatives and adjectives describing places

**2** Complete the sentences using comparative or superlative forms of the adjectives in brackets.

1 I love the Italian countryside. It's even _____ I expected. (picturesque)
2 Rio carnival is fantastic. It's probably _____ carnival in the world. (lively)
3 The tsunami hit some of the _____ beaches in Asia. (unspoilt)
4 Geneva is probably _____ place I've ever been to. (expensive)
5 Those old blocks of flats make the area look _____ . (ugly)
6 It's a residential area with nothing to do there. It's _____ part of the city. (dull)
7 I think it would look better if it were _____ . (modern)
8 They have stopped cars driving in the centre, so now it is much _____ . (polluted)
9 My mother-in-law cleaned the house. It's _____ than it has ever been before! (clean)
10 The town was so busy. It's much _____ than it was a few years ago. (touristy)

**3** Use the prompts in brackets to complete the second sentence so that it means the same as the first.

1 My old mp3 player is better than my new one.
  My new mp3 player _____ . (as)
2 London is more expensive than New York.
  New York _____ . (cheap)
3 More tourists visit Glasgow now than they did ten years ago.
  Glasgow _____ before. (touristy)
4 I have never seen a city which is more picturesque than Florence.
  Florence _____ . (most)
5 Los Angeles is more polluted than San Francisco.
  San Francisco _____ . (not)
6 Most cities are dirtier than Singapore.
  Singapore is _____ . (one)
7 More things happen in Shanghai nowadays.
  Shanghai _____ recently. (busier)
8 The west coast of the island has not had so many visitors.
  The west coast _____ . (unspoilt)

## Future possibility

**4** Write sentences using the prompts. Include the words in brackets.

1 We/see you/in the restaurant. (probably)
  _____

2 Do you think/she/say 'Yes'? (might)
  _____

3 I think/I/be late/for the lesson. (going)
  _____

4 You/need/to change money. (definitely not)
  _____

5 They/ask you/for your passport. (certainly)
  _____

6 We/not/get an answer/until tomorrow. (may)
  _____

7 I/call her again/in the morning. (definitely)
  _____

8 She/arrive/at any time. (could)
  _____

9 Helga/go/to Russia next year. (probably not)
  _____

10 He/accept/the job he was offered. (might not)
  _____

## Vocabulary

**5** Put the letters in the correct order to make words to complete the sentences.

1 She lives in a _____ of flats. (clokb)
2 It is a residential _____ . (eara)
3 Look out of the window. What a fantastic _____ ! (wiev)
4 They live a long way from the centre, in the _____ . (burssub)
5 There is a park near here, with a _____ for the children. (gorlandyup)
6 The office is on the _____ of town. (sutsorikt)
7 Shall we have breakfast on the _____ ? (clanybo)

**6** Add seven words to the text where necessary.

I recently went to visit my cousin in Tokyo, one the world's most bustling cities. He lives in a leafy residential area the outskirts of town. His block flats is actually not far the airport, and he came to pick me up when I arrived. In the car, he was apologising the fact that his flat wasn't as big people's homes in England. But in fact when we got there, I was surprised: his apartment was much bigger my studio flat in London!

**7** Choose the correct words in *italics*.

**Here is the news.**

(1) *Waves/Flooding* has caused damage to the island of Samaro, but fortunately nobody has been killed.

Environmentalists say (2) *weather/climate* change is responsible.

New research says that houses with (3) *insulated/ insulation* roofs are up to 45 percent cheaper to heat.

More people are now growing their own food than at any time in the last fifty years, a report says. The author of the report says that people want to be (4) *sufficient/self-sufficient* in order to save time and money. They also want to produce less (5) *house/ household* waste. And she also claims that people who grow their own food are 50 percent more likely to use (6) *solar/sun* panels, or some other way of generating their own electricity.

More news in an hour.

**8** The compound nouns in bold are in the wrong sentences. Rewrite the sentences putting the compound nouns in the correct sentences.

I have a ~~mobile phone~~ *sofa bed* in my sitting room, which guests sometimes sleep on.

1 It's cold in here. Let's turn on the **sofa bed.**
2 I don't have anything to wear because my clothes are all in the **central heating**.
3 Can I borrow your **bunk bed**? I need to call my office.
4 If I spend too long looking at a **washing machine**, I get headaches.
5 My brother and I shared a bedroom and slept in a **computer screen**.

**9** Find and correct four mistakes in the prefixes and suffixes in the sentences.

1 I find it annoying when people dispronounce my name.
2 She's really creatile, and she's always got good ideas.
3 You're always making careless mistakes.
4 We had a really enjoyible evening.
5 I don't understand why you unlike him so much!
6 St Petersburg is a really attractive city.

## How to...

**10** There is a word order mistake in five of the sentences. Find and correct the mistakes.

I ~~don't to like~~ complain, but ...

*I don't like to complain, but ...*

1 I'm to sorry hear that.
2 We must about that apologise.
3 My hope is to have three children.
4 I apologise do for the inconvenience.
5 I'm sorry, but it just isn't enough good.
6 My ambition is to become completely self-sufficient.
7 I have a dream lifelong of opening my own restaurant.

## Vocabulary | wealth and time

**1** In each sentence, two endings are possible, and one is not. Choose the answer that is not possible.

1 We've run out of time/life/money.
2 Don't go and see the film – it's not worth the cinema/time/money.
3 That man stole my money/bicycle/time.
4 We can save transport/time/money if we just walk there.
5 Could you lend me some money/some time/your mobile?
6 Joining a gym is a good way to spend your time/money/hobby.
7 She earned lots of money/some time/our thanks.
8 I always try to use my costs/money/time wisely.

## Vocabulary | phrasal verbs

**2** Complete the article with phrasal verbs from the box. Make sure you use the correct tense.

> break up    catch up    drop out    end up
> pick up    run out    work out

# Life-changer:

### Steve Riddell tells us how a bad time turned good

I was having the worst time of my life. I'd just (1) _____ with my girlfriend and (2) _____ of university. I needed to (3) _____ what I was going to do with the rest of my life. So I went travelling around South America. The idea was to keep travelling until I (4) _____ of money. After a few months I'd (5) _____ some Spanish words and made some friends in Colombia. We went our separate ways, but later I decided to (6) _____ with them in Cali. What a fantastic place! I (7) _____ living there for ten years!

## Grammar | question tags

**3** Complete the sentences with the question tags in the box.

> aren't I    aren't we    aren't you    didn't we
> don't they    hasn't she    will he    won't you

1 We're going home now, _____ ?
2 You'll be back tomorrow, _____ ?
3 She has eaten already, _____ ?
4 I'm on the list, _____ ?
5 You're from Ghana, _____ ?
6 He won't shoot, _____ ?
7 They work here, _____ ?
8 We stayed here before, _____ ?

**4** **a** Complete each sentence with a question tag. Then match the sentences (1–6) with the pictures (A–F).

1 This exam is hard, _____ ?
2 You aren't nervous, _____ ?
3 You can't play the violin, _____ ?
4 Chopsticks are easy to use, _____ ?
5 You haven't eaten spaghetti before, _____ ?
6 You've just arrived from somewhere cold, _____ ?

**b** Match the questions (1–6) in exercise 4a with the answers (a–f).

a A little bit. I don't like heights, you see.
b Yes, it is. And I forgot to revise.
c No, I can't. It's hard work, isn't it?
d No, it's the first time. But it's tasty.
e I have, yes. From Russia actually.
f Actually, I'm finding them quite hard.

## Pronunciation | intonation in question tags

**5** 🔊 12 Listen to the sentences from exercise 4. Does the speaker use ⟍⟋ or ⟋⟍ intonation?

## Listening

**6** **a** Nancy Bryant, a fraud prevention officer, is talking about how to stop financial crime. Read the definitions below before you listen.

> **fraud** *(n)* an illegal trick intended to deceive another person
>
> **fake** *(adj, v, n)* make something look like it is real when it is not

**b** 🔊 13 Listen to Parts 1, 2 and 3. Cover the audioscript. Number these topics in the order Nancy talks about them.

| | | | |
|---|---|---|---|
| 'phishing' | ☐ | her job | ☐ |
| advice for consumers | ☐ | Internet fraud | ☐ |
| investing your money | ☐ | shopping online | ☐ |
| identity fraud | ☐ | | |

**c** Listen to each part separately again, then answer the questions.

**Part 1**

1  What does Nancy do in her job?

2  Why is Internet fraud easier for criminals these days?

**Part 2**

3  What does Nancy say about cheap offers for Internet shoppers?

4  What four things should you never give over the Internet?

**Part 3**

5  Is online fraud currently rising or falling in the UK?

6  What advice does Nancy have for consumers?

**AUDIOSCRIPT**

**Part 1**

I: Nancy, fraud is becoming more and more common. Every day we hear of new cases of people losing large amounts of money.

N: That's right.

I: And your job is ... ?

N: My job is to tell the public what's happening, and explain how to stop fraud.

I: Right, and the main area you're working on now is Internet fraud I think, isn't it?

N: That's right. For criminals, Internet fraud is easier because it's so impersonal. In the old days they had to make fake cheques and to be actors. Nowadays though, they can steal money without ever even meeting their victims.

**Part 2**

I: Nancy, what can we actually do to prevent Internet fraud?

N: Lots of things. Firstly, be careful about shopping online. If someone offers you something incredibly cheap, then that's a dangerous sign. Or if you see an offer asking you to invest your money now, be careful. Most real investment opportunities don't work like this. They don't come looking for strangers over the Internet.

I: What about giving your details over the net?

N: Never give bank account numbers or passwords over the net.

I: Right, because then people could start spending your money?

N: Well, not just that. They can actually steal your identity as well. A lot of criminals have managed to get passports, even bank loans, by pretending to be someone else.

I: OK, so what can people do to prevent identity fraud?

N: Keep your details secure. Don't put your address or date of birth on any social networking sites, because criminals can use this information to pretend to be you.

**Part 3**

I: I've heard that online fraud is actually falling. Is this true?

N: Well, it's true that in the UK, less money is now being stolen each year through fraud on credit cards and debit cards.

I: So it's true then?

N: Well, yes and no – it all depends on how you understand the numbers.

I: How do you mean?

N: Well, phishing is actually on the increase.

I: Right, this is when you're asked for your card details online, but it's not from a genuine shop.

N: Yes, and it's not easy to know which websites are fake and which are genuine. So we're saying to people: if you're not sure, don't enter your details online.

## Vocabulary | personal qualities

**1** Match the sentence beginnings (1–7) with the sentence endings (a–g).

1 Managers have to be good
2 Actors need to have a sense
3 She's so ambitious – she wants
4 Our boss is very generous, and is
5 All workers should know their strengths
6 She's very confident and really believes
7 Architects need to

a of humour.
b with people.
c work long hours.
d and weaknesses.
e in her own ability.
f always giving us presents.
g to be the world's top pop star.

**2** Complete the job adverts with the words in the box.

> ambitious    figures    flexible    hours    humour

1 Wanted – staff to work in airport restaurant kitchen. Must be _____ – some work at night.

2 Are you a/an _____ person? Do you want to succeed, and earn $$$$$? Are you good at selling to customers by phone? Then we want to hear from you.

3 Are you good with _____ ? Can you add up the price of a round of drinks in your head? Would you like to serve thirsty customers?

4 We're looking for a dynamic person with a good sense of _____ to join our team on the door of Big Harry's Nightclub.

5 Stowton Hospital requires paramedic staff. Driving license essential. May need to work long _____ .

## Grammar | modals of obligation and prohibition

**3** Find and correct the mistakes in the sentences.

1 You must to come here now.
2 I've finished. What I should do now?
3 You don't must smoke in the office.
4 You haven't to wear a suit, but you can if you want to.
5 Shouldn't you to be at home now?
6 Am I have to buy a ticket?
7 She doesn't have to cleaning her room every day; only at weekends.
8 Our boss have to be in the office at 7:00 a.m.
9 I must going to the station now.
10 We are don't have to walk. We can take the car.

## Pronunciation | connected speech

**4 a** Read the sentences. Find and cross out one letter which you think won't be pronounced.

1 Don't do it!
2 Look at that dog!
3 Did Dave know?
4 You can't take that.
5 Why do you waste time?
6 My house has a red door.
7 You must get ready now.

**b** 🔊 14 Listen and check.

## Vocabulary | shopping

**5** Choose the correct answer to the questions, a or b.

1 Which phrase means 'something you bought, but which you hadn't planned to buy'?
   a An *impulse buy*       b A *bargain*

2 *Shopping around* means:
   a Buying lots of things
   b Trying to find the best price before buying something

3 If you take something you bought back to the shop and ask for your money back, what do you want?
   a A trolley                b A refund

4 Which preposition usually follows the phrase *spend money*?
   a on                       b of

5 What's the name for the part of a shop where you pay?
   a Price comparison website
   b Checkout

## How to... | report survey results

**6** Choose the correct words in *italics* to complete the text.

**I carried (1) *out/up* a survey to find out about the shopping habits of students at my university.**

(2) *Most of/Most of the* students I interviewed (87 percent) use the Internet to do their shopping at least once a month. Quite (3) *few/a few* of them were concerned about their money being stolen online, but (4) *hardly any of/hardly any* the people I interviewed (only 6 percent) (5) *talked/said* this had actually happened to them.

## Reading

**7 a** Read the article. Mark the sentences true (T) or false (F).

1 William Johnstone knew how to buy things over the Internet.
2 The person who was selling the aeroplane sent it to William's home.
3 Bill Davies thought he was going to win a lot of money.
4 Many other people had chosen the same winning numbers as Davies.
5 Zudan spent all of his lottery money in two months.
6 Zudan is sad because he is not rich now.
7 Samantha Brown knew there was some money hidden in the mattress.
8 Mr and Mrs Brown lost £18,000.

**b** Read the article again and choose the best meaning of these words and phrases, a or b.

1 To *blow money* means ...
   a to spend money intelligently.
   b to spend money quickly and foolishly.
2 *Go on a spending spree* means ...
   a to buy a lot of things very quickly.
   b to have an expensive holiday.
3 *Winnings* means ...
   a the money you save.
   b prize money.
4 *Jackpot* means ...
   a a large amount of money that you can win.
   b a pot where you keep money.
5 *In debt* means ...
   a without a job.
   b you owe (have to pay) money to someone, or to an institution.
6 *Life savings* means ...
   a money for saving your life (if you have to go to hospital).
   b all the money you have saved.

# How not to get rich quick

William Johnstone, aged seven, went on an Internet shopping website, and, using his mother's credit card, bought himself an aeroplane. No, not a toy aeroplane. A jet-fighter. Fortunately, the seller realised there was something wrong when he asked for the delivery address. Flat number 53 in downtown Detroit was not the answer he was expecting. In this case, not a penny was spent, but there are plenty of other cases of people blowing lots of money very quickly, very stupidly.

Californian Bill Davies didn't even get that far. When he saw that he had the winning numbers in his local lottery, he immediately ordered a Mercedes, booked a family holiday in Hawaii and had a champagne dinner for friends and family. When he went to pick up his winnings, he found that 9,022 others had also won first prize! His share of the jackpot was $40.

Jack Zudan won nearly $1,000,000 on the lottery in January 2011. By May, he had $400 left. 'I got a bit excited,' said the builder, twenty-four. He went on a spending spree and bought six cars, including two for friends. Of those six, by May he had already crashed two, and his friend crashed a third in June. Fortunately, Zudan was able to return to his old job. 'It was fun while it lasted,' he said, 'but I'm happier working with my mates.'

When 76-year-old Samantha Brown realised her husband was in debt, she decided to sell as many things as possible, including an old mattress. A few weeks later her husband nervously asked her where the mattress was. Hidden inside it were his life savings of £18,000. They managed to find the mattress but not the money which, strangely, 'had taken a walk'.

## Grammar | Zero and First Conditionals with *if/when/unless/as soon as*

**1 a** Choose the correct words in *italics*.

1 *As soon as/Unless* you arrive, will you call me?

2 *Unless/As soon as* I can, I'll go home and get some sleep.

3 *As soon as/Unless* you work harder, you won't pass the exam.

4 *If/When* you wake up tomorrow, you'll see snow.

5 *As soon as/If* you like action films, you'll love *Fast Escape*.

6 *If/Unless* we find a taxi right now, we'll miss the plane.

7 *Unless/If* I see Dave, I'll tell him you called.

8 *When/Unless* you go on holiday, will you send me a postcard?

9 *If/Unless* you take an umbrella, you won't get wet.

10 *When/Unless* you get home, we'll watch a DVD.

11 *As soon as/If* you get there, you should check into your room.

12 *When/Unless* you're nicer to Mum, she won't pick you up tonight.

**b** Match the replies (a–l) with the statements (1–12) in exercise 1a.

a Look. Here's one coming now.

b Sure. I'll give you a call when I land.

c What? But the exam will be easy!

d I've already seen it – it was rubbish!

e Is that what the weather forecast said?

f Good point. Can I borrow yours then?

g OK. Which one do you fancy watching?

h Thanks, and can you ask him to ring me?

i Yes, I'm sure you'll be really tired by then.

j I don't do that any more – why don't you read my holiday blog?

k Fine! Then I'll walk home.

l That's a great idea. Then we can leave our suitcases there.

**2** Complete the sentences with the verbs in brackets in the correct tense. Include the pronouns where necessary.

1 **A:** I _____ (not/be) home for dinner unless _____ (finish) my work.

   **B:** As soon as you _____ (know) if you're coming, _____ (phone) me?

2 **A:** Where _____ (you/go) if you _____ (take) a holiday?

   **B:** If _____ (have) enough money, I _____ (visit) my aunt in Canada.

3 **A:** When you _____ (graduate), _____ (you/become) a professor?

   **B:** If I _____ (find) a job, it _____ (not/be) as a professor. I'll be a research assistant first.

4 **A:** We _____ (be) stuck here for hours unless we _____ (turn) off the motorway.

   **B:** If we _____ (not/find) a restaurant, we _____ (die) of hunger.

**3** Match the sentence beginnings (1–8) with the sentence endings (a–h).

1 If the students get under 50 percent in the final exam,

2 We won't give you a refund

3 If you have problems remembering names,

4 Unless you pay for the ticket within four days,

5 We will continue to deliver the magazine

6 The committee will inform you

7 When you subscribe to News24.com,

8 The taxi will pick you up

a as soon as it makes its decision.

b unless you bring the receipt.

c you will benefit from the course in Memory Development.

d we will email you a secret password.

e they won't be able to move to the next level of the class.

f when you finish work.

g our office won't be able to guarantee you a seat.

h unless you tell us that you no longer wish to receive it.

# How to... | ask for clarification

**4** Put the words in the correct order to make sentences.

1  not/I'm/Sorry,/you./with
2  explain/Could/again?/you that
3  I'm/quite/sorry,/I/get/that./didn't
4  mean/Do/can't/you/you/it?/afford
5  you/Are/saying/too/it's/that/expensive?
6  egotistical?/So/you're/what/saying/is/I'm/that

# Vocabulary | confusing words

**5** **a** Tick (✓) the sentences which are true.

1  A coin is metal money.  ☐
2  A note is paper money.  ☐
3  A library is a place that can lend you books.  ☐
4  A penalty you have to pay as a punishment (e.g. for not having a train ticket) is called a fee.  ☐
5  Another word for a discount is a refund.  ☐
6  You can buy now and pay later if you have a credit card.  ☐
7  A receipt is a piece of paper asking you to pay a certain amount.  ☐
8  The cost of a journey by public transport is called a change.  ☐

**b** Correct the four false statements in exercise 5a by replacing the incorrect words with a word from the box.

( bill   fare   fine   reduction )

# Reading

**6** **a** Read the article and tick (✓) the best heading, 1, 2 or 3.

1  The dangers of advertising
2  Using computers to follow animals
3  The future of the personalised ad

**b** Which paragraph tells us ...

a  what RFID is?
b  about potential problems of RFID?
c  how RFID is being used in Japan?
d  how shops intend to use RFID?

**c** Read the article again. Mark the sentences true (T) or false (F) or not given (NG).

RFID tags are ...

1  very small.
2  used for following the movements of animals.
3  used as weapons by the US Department of Defence.
4  in all clothes.
5  used by some commercial companies already.
6  dangerous for the health of workers.

---

**1** If you happen to be shopping in the Ginza district of Tokyo, you might get a message on your mobile telling you which of the shops you're near has a sale on at the moment. But how do the shops know to contact you? How do they know where you are?

**2** The answer is RFID – radio frequency identification. RFID is in many ways a great idea. How does it work? Tiny computer chips (or 'tags') are attached to objects, clothes or packaging. These chips can be read by a central computer network. If you want to find your lost dog or to research the movements of ants, RFID is very helpful. This is what researchers at Bristol University did in 2009. Just put the tag on the animal and watch from a safe distance. RFID has commercial uses too. Delta Airlines uses it to track luggage and the US Department of Defense uses it to count its weapons and vehicles.

**3** So how can RFID be used in advertising? Well, imagine your clothes have an RFID tag. Every time you enter the shopping mall a scanner 'reads' your name, age and buying habits. It knows which shampoo you buy, which bread you prefer, the size of your feet. The scanner then uses this information to target you with special offers. Just a few years ago, this sounded like science fiction, but it's becoming more and more common.

**4** So, what's the problem? The problem is that great technology is often used for less great purposes. RFID could easily be used to track people instead of products. The boss may decide to track his workers – to see who spends their time smoking outside or taking long lunch breaks. The government may decide it wants to see which books you are reading or which political gatherings you attend. As all shoppers know, everything costs something. The cost of RFID may be your privacy.

## Question tags

**1** Complete the sentences using a question tag. Use the prompts in brackets.

*The sky is black and it's raining heavily. (horrible day)*

*It's a horrible day, isn't it?*

1 Your friend is looking thinner than usual. (lose weight)
You've _____ ?

2 You're listening to a boring radio show. (not very interesting)
This _____ ?

3 You think your friend secretly ate your last chocolate. (ate)
You _____ ?

4 You are saying goodbye to a friend who is going travelling. (write to me)
You will _____ ?

5 You are looking for your sunglasses. (see)
You haven't _____ ?

6 Your friend is at your barbecue. You think she is a vegetarian. (eat meat)
You don't _____ ?

7 You are checking that your friend knows how to drive. (can)
You _____ ?

8 You are talking about your first ever teacher. (wonderful)
She was _____ ?

9 You check that your friend still runs regularly. (every day)
You still _____ ?

## Modals of obligation and prohibition

**2** Each sentence has a mistake. Either add a word or cross out a word.

*We should to bring flowers, shouldn't we?*

1 I need to send Judith an email, I?

2 We mustn't have write in the book, must we?

3 They shouldn't arrive so late, should not they?

4 He has go to class now, doesn't he?

5 She doesn't have to be wear a hat, does she?

6 I must invite Samuel, I?

7 You have to memorise the password, haven't don't you?

8 None of us has should be worried, should we?

## Zero and First Conditional with *if/when/unless/as soon as*

**3** Complete the second sentence so that it means the same as the first. Use two to four words.

1 Unless we eat early, there won't be any food left. (If)
_____ eat early, there won't be any food left.

2 Immediately after you arrive, you will receive a ticket. (as)
You will be given a ticket _____ you arrive.

3 It's not necessary for us to book a place on the course. (have)
We _____ book a place on the course.

4 If I drink too much coffee, I'll be awake all night. (be)
_____ able to sleep if I drink too much coffee.

5 It's a good idea to call the office first. (phone)
We _____ the office first.

6 Playing ball games is forbidden here. (mustn't)
You _____ ball games here.

7 She can take the test if she wants to, but it isn't obligatory. (have)
She _____ take the test.

8 He won't come to the meeting unless it's really necessary. (come)
He _____ to the meeting if it's really necessary.

9 You should wash your hands before you eat. (eat)
You _____ before washing your hands.

10 Young children who do lots of exercise get tired easily.
Young children get tired easily _____ lots of exercise. (if)

**4** Choose the correct words in *italics*.

1 Unless we *buy/will buy* a phone card, we *won't/will* be able to call home.

2 *If/As soon as* you don't like meat, you *won't/don't* enjoy this restaurant.

3 When you *will pass/pass* the cinema, you *will to/will* see an Internet café. Turn left there.

4 *Will you/You will* call me as soon as you *will know/know* the answer?

5 *Unless/If* they don't take credit cards, we *won't/can't* be able to pay.

6 It *will/doesn't* be great for Europe when these countries *join/will join* the EU.

7 Technology *will/won't* develop if we *put/will put* money into it.

8 *When/As* you reach the age of seventeen, we *will organise/organise* driving lessons for you.

9 *Unless/When* that bag weighs less than ten kilos, you *won't/will* be able to take it.

10 *Won't you/You won't* fall off your bicycle if you *won't/don't* use your hands?

## Vocabulary

**5** **a** Complete the phrasal verbs from the unit in the sentences.

1 It's hard – I can't work _____ what to do.

2 He dropped out _____ college in the first term.

3 She's just broken up _____ her boyfriend, so she's upset.

4 That's all – I'm afraid we've run out _____ time, so I'll see you all again next week.

5 Bob and I were really god friends, but ended _____ having a huge argument.

6 Watching films in English helps me pick _____ a few new words.

7 Did you grow _____ in this area?

8 She's really good at making _____ funny stories, isn't she?

**b** Match the replies (a–h) with the sentences (1–8) in exercise 5a.

a Yes, I find it helps me too.

b It's easy. Let me show you.

c Thanks for the lesson. Bye.

d Oh dear. Didn't he like his course?

e And how do you get on with him now?

f Has she? How long were they together?

g She is, yes. I don't know where she gets her ideas from.

h Yes, I've always lived here.

**6** Tick (✓) the correct sentence in each pair, a or b.

1 a I have an interesting work. ☐
  b I have an interesting job. ☐

2 a Remind me to buy milk tomorrow. ☐
  b Remember me to buy milk tomorrow. ☐

3 a I don't want to lose this show. ☐
  b I don't want to miss this show. ☐

4 a Can you lend me some money? ☐
  b Can you borrow me some money? ☐

5 a He robbed a famous museum. ☐
  b He stole a famous museum. ☐

6 a Don't drive too fast, or you'll have to pay a fare. ☐
  b Don't drive too fast, or you'll have to pay a fine. ☐

7 a How was your travel? ☐
  b How was your trip? ☐

8 a Skiing is always fun. ☐
  b Skiing is always funny. ☐

**7** Complete the phrases in the sentences.

1 The definition of a b_____ t_____ i_____ is a product that is more expensive than other things in the same shop.

2 It was reduced from €96 to €32, so I think it was really g_____ v_____ f_____ money.

3 I never buy anything until I've shopped around and checked the p_____ c_____ websites to see how cheap I can get it.

4 You've got to have a good s_____ o_____ h_____ in this job, and if you do, you can have a good laugh at work.

5 I don't use much cash, as I pay for almost everything with my d_____ c_____ .

6 I studied maths at university, and I'm quite g_____ w_____ f_____ , so I became an accountant.

7 My mum has to w_____ l_____ h_____ in her job. Yesterday she was at work for thirteen hours.

8 I went into the shop for some batteries, and came out with a flatscreen TV – it was an i_____ b_____.

## How to...

**8** Read the dialogue between a schoolboy and his mother. Find and correct six mistakes in the dialogue.

A: We did a survey at school today.

B: Sorry, I'm not with your. What do you mean?

A: We asked each other survey questions in class.

B: Oh I see. What are you saying is you interviewed each other – is that right?

A: Exactly. And most of the people in the class told that they can go out in the evenings.

B: Well, do you means 'every evening'?

A: Yes, of course. And hardly any the students said they have to come home before 10:00 p.m.

B: OK, OK. I think I understand. Do you saying that you want to go out again tonight?

A: Oh, well yes actually. Can I go round to Marta's? She's having a party ...

## Vocabulary | free time

**1** Use the clues to complete the crossword.

**Across**

3 indoor raquet game with a small ball
8 Japanese martial art
9 the thing in the middle of a tennis court
10 spending time with friends
14 taking pictures

**Down**

1 the world's most popular sport
2 things for protecting the eyes
3 sea sport with a board
4 hard hat for cyclists, horseriders, etc.
5 sports shoes
6 thing that cyclists and horseriders sit on
7 thing used to hit the ball in tennis and squash
11 exercise class with music
12 thing needed for chess and for surfing
13 riding a bike

## How to... | describe your response to a picture

**2** Complete the text by adding the words from the box in the correct place.

> if   makes   me   to   way

I can't draw or paint now, but when I was a child I made pictures all the time. I've got one I painted when I was about six years old. I think it's meant show me and my family. I still have vivid memories of the day when I painted it. I like the we're all smiling in the picture, and it looks as we're having a great time. Every time I look at it it me feel cheerful. It reminds of the time when I was a little boy, and when everything was fun.

## Grammar | Present Perfect Continuous and Present Perfect Simple

**3** Choose the correct words in *italics*.

1 She's *finished/been finishing* her book. She wrote the final page last night.
2 I've *watched/been watching* this film for an hour now and I don't understand anything!
3 I'm exhausted because I've *worked/been working* since 5:00 a.m.
4 We've *gone/been going* to samba classes since June. It's fun. Why don't you come?
5 How long have you *known/been knowing* Clara?
6 Your tennis is getting better. Have you *practised/been practising*?
7 That was the best film I've ever *seen/been seeing*.

**4** Use the prompts to complete the dialogues with the Present Perfect Simple or Continuous. Write two, three or four words in each space.

1 A: I met Ravi ten years ago.
   B: So you _____ Ravi for ten years. (know)
2 A: Can't you find your glasses?
   B: No. I _____ them for hours. (look for)
3 A: You look tired.
   B: I _____ since eight in the morning. (run)
4 A: Where have you been?
   B: I _____ on my computer in my room. (play)
5 A: Do you like my new CD?
   B: I _____ it yet, so I don't know. (hear)
6 A: She's got a driving lesson tomorrow.
   B: How long _____ to drive? (learn)
7 A: I'm having a party tomorrow.
   B: How many people _____ ? (invite)

## Reading

**5** Match the stories (1–3) with the pictures (A–C).

Why is it that teenagers and adults get bored so easily, but young children are able to think of endless ways to keep themselves entertained? Three people tell us about what they did as young children.

5 **1) Anthony**
Well, when I was young my mum and dad were always playing classical music on CD. I liked the noise of this music – well, I think I just liked any noise basically. So I always tried to join in. I was only about three – much too young to play the piano or any other musical
10 instrument. So I went to the kitchen, found a saucepan and a couple of wooden spoons. Then I took **them** to the room where my parents were listening to old composers like Brahms or Beethoven. And I just started hitting the saucepans with the spoons. I loved it, and spent ages doing this. I think it drove my parents crazy – they started
15 taking me out into the garden and leaving me there to make all this awful noise! Still, I enjoyed myself.

**2) José**
In my childhood we didn't have many toys and things. We managed without a computer or anything like that. Didn't need **one** really –
20 my brother and I were really creative, and just invented our own games all the time. My favourite was using my hands and feet to climb up the inside of doorways. I loved getting right up to the top and then jumping back down onto the floor. We played games to see who could climb up to the top the quickest, and who could stay
25 there for the longest.

**3) Sergey**
Like José, there weren't a lot of toys in my family. But we did have quite a few dogs. Of course, when you're a very young child, a dog seems like a huge animal. So my younger sister and I, we used
30 to sit on them and ride them like horses! No helmets, no saddles, we just sat on them, and tried to make the dogs take us round the house! I was never very good at **it** – I think I weighed too much. I usually fell off, then just went and had some cake! But my sister became really good.

**6** **a** Match the questions (1–3) with the answers (a–c).
Who …
1 had competitions with other family members?
2 annoyed the other people in his family?
3 was too big to do something well?

a Anthony
b Sergey
c José

**b** Read the stories again. Write true (T) or false (F).
1 The introduction says that little children are good at thinking of things to do. ☐
2 Anthony was learning to play the piano. ☐
3 Anthony talks about playing inside and outside. ☐
4 José had lots of computer games as a child. ☐
5 José and his brother created their own games. ☐
6 Sergey wore a helmet when he was riding. ☐
7 Sergey says he was a better rider than his sister. ☐

**c** What do the words in **bold** in the text refer to?
1 them (line 11)
   a parents
   b saucepan and spoons
   c composers
2 one (line 19)
   a childhood
   b computer
   c brother
3 it (line 32)
   a riding dogs
   b weighing his sister
   c making cake

## Pronunciation | weak forms

**7** 🔘 15 Listen and tick (✓) the sentences you hear, a or b.
1 a John's been working. ☐
  b John's working. ☐
2 a Have you been eating? ☐
  b Have you eaten? ☐
3 a I've painted it. ☐
  b I painted it. ☐
4 a I've been reading. ☐
  b I'm reading. ☐
5 a We lost. ☐
  b We've lost. ☐
6 a She's finished. ☐
  b She hasn't finished. ☐
7 a Are you seeing her? ☐
  b Have you seen her? ☐
8 a I've done the work. ☐
  b I haven't done the work. ☐

## Grammar | -ing and infinitive

**1 a** Read what Jenny Schubert says about her work. What is her job?

1 writer     3 book editor

2 cook      4 English teacher

I love _seeing_ (see) a book begin to develop, and I try (1) _____ (work) closely with the author. During the early stages, I invite the author (2) _____ (have) dinner with me at home. We usually manage (3) _____ (discuss) the book while eating.

It sounds strange, but I'd like (4) _____ (read) more for pleasure. I don't seem (5) _____ (find) the time to read books outside my field of work, and I hate (6) _____ (start) books when I don't have time to finish them.

I enjoy (7) _____ (speak) to young writers and I advise them (8) _____ (read) as much as they can. I also tell them (9) _____ (write) from the heart, about things that are important to them. I sometimes agree (10) _____ (look) at the work of a new author if I expect (11) _____ (enjoy) the book, but I refuse (12) _____ (read) new work if it's full of spelling mistakes or badly presented.

**b** Complete the sentences with the -ing or infinitive form of the verbs in brackets.

**2** Complete the sentences with the -ing or infinitive form of the verbs in the box.

> beat   get   have   play (x2)   speak   study
> watch   write

What do the stars do in their free time?

1 Bill Clinton adores _____ the saxophone.

2 Gwyneth Paltrow loves languages and is learning _____ Spanish.

3 Ronaldinho is trying _____ better at karaoke – he has a machine in his house.

4 Robbie Williams is often invited _____ football in celebrity matches.

5 Film star Keira Knightley enjoys _____ films.

6 Kylie Minogue loves Scrabble and regularly manages _____ the writer, Salman Rushdie!

7 Serena Williams designs clothes and would like _____ her own fashion company.

8 Angelina Jolie finished _____ to be a pilot in 2004. She now flies her own plane.

## Vocabulary | describing pastimes

**3** Use the clues to complete the crossword.

1 A _____ is a person who really likes one sports team. (synonym = fan)

2 The _____ is the tune in a piece of music.

3 The words of a song are called the _____ .

4 A _____ is a person who really likes one sports team. (synonym = supporter)

5 The _____ is the story that is told in a novel or film.

6 The verb 'to _____ ' means to act the role of an important character in a film.

7 An _____ is a CD or download of music, usually about ten or twelve songs, and usually by the same artist.

8 To _____ in football means to score a goal, so that the score is equal, e.g. 1–1 or 2–2.

9 An album with music from a film is called a _____ .

10 A person in a film or novel is called a _____ .

11 A book (or other product) which lots of people buy is called a _____ .

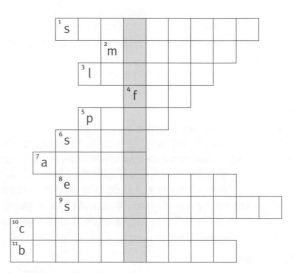

**4** Choose the correct options to complete the text.

My favourite (1) _____ is Nick Hornby. Every book of his is a real (2) _____ – they're not thrillers or anything, his (3) _____ are just ordinary people who live ordinary lives.

His novel *High Fidelity* is (4) _____ in a record shop, and the (5) _____ character is the manager, Rob. He knows everything about music – if someone told him the name of a song, he could say which (6) _____ it was on. He could probably tell you all the (7) _____ as well. *High Fidelity* was made into a film, (8) _____ John Cusack as Rob, who gives a brilliant (9) _____ .

| | | | |
|---|---|---|---|
| 1 | **A** best-seller | **B** author |
| 2 | **A** page-turner | **B** chapter |
| 3 | **A** characters | **B** actors |
| 4 | **A** written | **B** set |
| 5 | **A** primary | **B** leading |
| 6 | **A** melody | **B** album |
| 7 | **A** single | **B** lyrics |
| 8 | **A** playing | **B** starring |
| 9 | **A** performance | **B** act |

## Pronunciation | sounds and spelling: *a*

**5** **a** Look at the pronunciation of 'a' in the groups of words. <u>Underline</u> the odd one out.

| | *page* | *game* | *change* | *match* |
|---|---|---|---|---|
| 1 | band | album | stage | catchy |
| 2 | character | play | fan | abandoned |
| 3 | hate | stand | fantastic | vampires |
| 4 | based | gave | straight | shadow |

**b** 🔘 16 Listen and check.

## Listening

**6** 🔘 17 Listen to four conversations comparing films and comic books. Complete the notes in the table.

| Speaker | Title of film/ comic book | Opinion |
|---|---|---|
| 1 Denise | *X-Men Origins* | The film was _____ than the comic book. She loved the _____ . |
| 2 Ahmed | _____ | He preferred the _____ . The star looked too _____ . |
| 3 Eliza | *Batman: Under the Red Hood* | The comic is dark but the film is _____ . She loved the performance of _____ . |
| 4 Glynn | _____ | He likes the comic and the film. He also loves the _____ . He doesn't like the _____ as much. |

**AUDIOSCRIPT**

**1**

**Denise:** I've recently seen the *X-Men Origins* film, which I really liked.

**Interviewer:** Oh yes? What did you like about it?

**Denise:** I thought it was much better than the comic book. I loved the action.

**2**

**Ahmed:** Um ... I saw *Spiderman 3*. But I didn't like it that much.

**Interviewer:** Did you prefer the comic?

**Ahmed:** Yeah, I much preferred the comic to the film. In the comic, the characters are more real, whereas ... um ... in the film, I didn't really like the actor who played Spiderman, the star ... what's his name ... is it Toby Maguire?

**Interviewer:** Toby Maguire, I think, yes.

**Ahmed:** He looked too young.

**3**

**Interviewer:** You saw the *Batman* film, didn't you?

**Eliza:** *Under the Red Hood?* I loved it.

**Interviewer:** Really? More than the comic?

**Eliza:** The comic is ... like ... really dark, set in this dark city, and it's all really tragic and everything, but the film is kind of funny. And I just loved Bruce Greenwood's performance as Batman.

**4**

**Glynn:** I think both the Superman comic book and the film were great.

**Interviewer:** Yeah, me too.

**Glynn:** And I love the soundtrack.

**Interviewer:** Yeah, it's great, isn't it?

**Glynn:** It's one of the things I remember most about the film, actually. Y'know, that music when he's flying above the city.

**Interviewer:** Yeah.

**Glynn:** The sequels aren't so good, but the first film's a classic.

## Vocabulary | food

**1** Find the six words connected with cooking in the wordsquare.

| b | s | c | f | a | r | t | s | i |
|---|---|---|---|---|---|---|---|---|
| o | t | g | r | i | l | l | e | d |
| i | u | r | i | q | w | f | r | i |
| l | f | g | e | e | r | d | v | k |
| e | f | e | d | d | f | p | e | j |
| d | e | f | b | a | k | e | d | t |
| d | d | n | w | w | m | d | s | g |

## Grammar | countable and uncountable nouns

**2** Find and correct the mistakes in four of the sentences.

1 I love your trousers – where did you get it?
2 Would you like a coffee?
3 I've got a little of time next week – shall we meet then?
4 Can I borrow that scissors, please?
5 There wasn't enough room for me in the car, so I had to walk.
6 I need to buy some new furnitures for my flat.
7 The strawberry ice cream was beautifully prepared.
8 Shall we have some rice for lunch?

**3** Choose the correct options to complete the recipe.

### How to make
# aubergine bake

This is a simple, delicious dish which doesn't take (1)_____ preparation.
You need 2 large aubergines, 4 tomatoes, 2 onions, 1 green pepper, garlic, 2 boiled eggs, cheese, oregano and salt.

Cut the aubergines into slices and leave them in salty water for 20 minutes. Slice the tomatoes, onions, green pepper and eggs. Grate the cheese.

Take a large tray and spread (2)_____ butter on it. Place (3)_____ pieces of aubergine on the tray, add (4)_____ garlic, and (5)_____ little bit of salt. Next, add the tomatoes, onions, pepper and (6)_____ cheese.

Repeat the steps adding another layer of the same ingredients. Put the sliced egg on top with (7)_____ pepper. Add (8)_____ of cheese this time and a couple of spoonfuls of oregano. Bake for 30 minutes.

| 1 | A a | B a lot | C much | D many |
|---|---|---|---|---|
| 2 | A some | B a | C much | D many |
| 3 | A much | B few | C a | D a few |
| 4 | A a | B lots of | C much | D a few |
| 5 | A – | B a | C the | D some |
| 6 | A a | B much | C some | D lot of |
| 7 | A some | B few | C little | D lots |
| 8 | A little | B many | C some | D lots |

## How to... | describe a restaurant

**4** Find and correct the nine spelling mistakes in the text.

**U Babci Maliny...** is my favourite restarant. It's near the main squaire in Krakow in Poland. It specalises in tradisional Polish food. The menu is very varried – you can have meat, fish, lots of vegetarian dishes as well as desserts. It gets very lively and noisy during the daytime, when it's full of locals as well as tourists. They come in their hundreds for the beatifully prepared food, freindly efficiant service and reesonable prices.

## Vocabulary | explaining what you mean

**5** **a** Correct the mistakes in the sentences.

1 It's a type machine you use for cooking things fast.

2 It's kind of game that uses pieces like kings and queens.

3 It's the stuffing you find on the ground after a freezing night.

4 It's something you use for boil water to make tea.

5 They are made by rubber and you put them on your wheels.

6 It's a stick type of tape that you can use to attach paper to a wall.

**b** Match the words (a–f) with the definitions (1–6) in exercise 5a.

a chess    c kettle    e microwave

b car tyres    d sellotape    f ice

## Reading

**6** **a** Read the descriptions of some people. Then read about the restaurants. Match the people (1–5) with the restaurants (a–e).

1 Brett and Matthew like hot, spicy dishes. They have travelled a lot, and they love South American or Asian food. ☐

2 The Wilkinsons like cheap, fast food, American food in particular. ☐

3 Mr and Mrs Lewsey like expensive European food and excellent wine. They want to go to a quiet, comfortable restaurant, not too far from the town centre. ☐

4 Dave and Jessie live on the coast. They are vegetarians, but they sometimes eat fish. They like cheap, cheerful restaurants. ☐

5 Megan and Sian like Italian food. The restaurant must be easy to reach and near the centre of the city. They like eating out on Sundays. ☐

a Cucina Romana is a modern restaurant specialising in pasta and pizza. Prices vary from £5.00 for our oven-baked calzone to £14.50 for our Seafood Deluxe pasta with shrimp and lobster. Free parking. Wheelchair access. Open daily 1:00 p.m. until midnight.

b Come and get it at MacBurgles Rapido! Hamburger, chips and fizzy drink for just £2.99. Family packs for just £8.99. If you have to wait more than ten minutes, we give you a free meal! Over the Christmas period, book our special Party Room for kids. Call 0207 676 2919 for bookings.

c Taste of the Taj Indian restaurant. Central London. Curries, chicken tikka masala. Excellent quality using fresh herbs and spices. Recommended by the *Orion Food Guide*: 'An outstanding eating experience.'

d Fisherman's Wharf is a friendly fish restaurant situated at the harbour, just twenty minutes from the centre of Hoban. Serving a wide variety of fish, we can guarantee freshness. All fish are caught locally. On Sundays try our special Seafood Combo of prawns, cod and squid for an unforgettable meal, at just £3.50.

'Fisherman's Wharf is fantastic value.' (*Hoban Enquirer*)

'Great service, great food!' (*City Entertainment Guide*, January 2005)

e Bistro Moderne This elegant, exclusive restaurant serves French, Spanish and Italian food. Our extensive cellar has over 400 wines for you to choose from. Prices from £70.00 per person. Open Monday to Saturday 7:00 – 11:30.

**b** Which restaurants …

1 tell you where they are? _____ and _____

2 offer special deals? _____ and _____

3 tell you when they are open? _____ and _____

4 tell you who has recommended them? _____ and _____

5 serve seafood? _____ and _____

6 serve meals for under £4.00? _____ and _____

# Review and consolidation unit 5

## Present Perfect Simple and Continuous

**1** Complete the sentences with the Present Perfect Simple or the Present Perfect Continuous form of the verbs in brackets.

1 _____ (you not/finish) your work yet? You're really slow!
2 There's chocolate all over your mouth! _____ (you/eat) ice cream again?!
3 You look bored. _____ (you/read) that book about nuclear physics? It's very long, isn't it?
4 I _____ (ask) her for my book six times, and she still hasn't returned it.
5 I'm exhausted. I _____ (study) all night and I still have to do one more essay!
6 It's cold in here because the window _____ (be) open all day.
7 The children are really tired. They _____ (ski) all morning.
8 We _____ (start) going to yoga classes. It's a great way to deal with stress.
9 There it is! I _____ (look) for that book for three weeks!
10 There's no paint left. We _____ (use) it all on the wall.

## countable and uncountable nouns/-*ing* and infinitive

**2** Complete the sentences with the -*ing* or infinitive form of the verbs in brackets, and choose the correct word in *italics*.

1 I enjoy _____ (cook) and I always use *few/a lot/ a lot of* garlic.
2 I didn't manage _____ (find out) anything. Did you find *any/many/a lot* information?
3 She really wants _____ (talk) to you. She needs *some/an/a few* advice.
4 I'm looking forward to _____ (meet) you. I've heard *a couple/so much/so many* good things about you.
5 There's something I'd like _____ (tell) you! It's *a/–/a few* good news.
6 They invited us _____ (go) on holiday with them, but it cost *too lot/too many/too much* money.
7 She finished _____ (write) the book years ago, but it took *few/many/much* years to find a publisher.
8 We don't mind _____ (look after) Sammy. Does he like *a/–/little* chocolate?
9 I can't stand _____ (run). It's even worse in *a/too/–* bad weather.
10 He refused _____ (eat) his vegetables. He wanted *an/few/little* ice cream instead!

## -*ing* and infinitive

**3** In each sentence, two endings are possible, and one is incorrect. Cross out the sentence ending which is not correct.

1 I began
 A to cry.
 B playing the violin.
 C play tennis.
2 I'd like
 A a coffee, please.
 B going home now.
 C to find a new job.
3 She tried
 A writing down new words.
 B to swim.
 C bake a cake.
4 We expect
 A make some money.
 B good weather.
 C to be there at 6:00.
5 Don't forget
 A me.
 B buy milk.
 C to clean the car.
6 We agreed
 A to start at 4:15.
 B with the doctor.
 C working together.
7 I stopped
 A to have a drink.
 B play with the dog.
 C writing poems years ago.
8 He remembered
 A dance all night.
 B meeting you last year.
 C to bring the presents.
9 She can't stand
 A watching TV.
 B do exercise.
 C vegetables.
10 Last year the team started
 A become popular.
 B winning.
 C to attract support.

**4** Put the words in the correct order to make sentences.

1 a/She's/subject/years./for/studying/the/of/been/couple

_____

2 of/heard/Mark./lot/I've/interesting/a/about/stories

_____

3 have/of/All/working/hard./been/you/very

_____

4 I've/for/coming/been/here/years./many

_____

5 time/in/spent/hasn't/Brazil./much/He

_____

6 Prague/of/us/A/stayed/few/before./in/have

_____

7 days/been/She's/taking/many/work./off/too

_____

8 some/to/He's/find/information./trying/been

_____

9 days./haven't/I/for/few/seen/you/a

_____

10 doing/has/of/My/today/been/mother/lot/gardening./a

_____

# Vocabulary

**5** Complete the words to match the definitions.

1 activity to keep the body flexible; sometimes uses music: a_____

2 physical activity that is good for your body: e_____

3 slow running: j_____

4 Japanese martial art: k_____

5 spending time with other people: s_____

6 moving a boat through water: s_____

7 something you use to hit the ball in tennis: r_____

8 something you sit on when you ride a horse: s_____

9 special shoes you use to do exercise: t_____

10 something you use to protect your eyes when you swim: g_____

**6** Match the words (1–8) with the definitions (a–h).

1 sound effects
2 audience
3 applause
4 is set
5 dialogue
6 sequel
7 heart throb
8 performance

a the act of presenting a play, dance or other form of entertainment

b the people watching a performance

c recorded sounds in a film, on the radio or in a play

d takes place

e a book or film which continues the story of a previous book or film

f the sound made by people watching a performance

g a conversation between characters in a book or play

h a man who is very attractive to women

**7** Choose the correct definition of the underlined word, a or b.

1 I don't like roadside restaurants – they're too noisy.
   a next to a road      b like a road

2 Marinate the chicken in olive oil and salt for three to four hours before baking.
   a fry in oil
   b leave food in flavouring before cooking

3 'Golabki', a Polish dish, is a cabbage leaf stuffed with rice and meat.
   a filled      b flavoured

4 I had chicken pie and chips for lunch.
   a a kind of chicken      b a kind of dish

5 The food in that restaurant is absolutely delicious – you should try it.
   a very tasty      b very expensive

6 I need to wash the tablecloth, because I spilt coffee on it.
   a material covering a table   b a dining table

# How to...

**8** **a** Quickly read the text. What is it?

1 a complaint about a bad meal
2 a review of an unusual restaurant
3 a description of a restaurant the writer visited as a child

**b** Correct the text by adding one word to each sentence.

There's a lovely restaurant the centre of the city where I live. It's called The Trout, and, unsurprisingly, it specialises seafood. When you walk in, you think you're in wrong place because you see lots of people cooking. It actually looks as you've come into the kitchen by mistake! It's famous being the city's only restaurant where you actually cook your own food! The smell is lovely – it reminds me my mother's kitchen when I was a child. I love going there, and I really like way you can cook whatever you want. You choose the ingredients need. Last time, I burnt fish, not great. But the prices reasonable, and it has a very relaxing atmosphere.

## Vocabulary | holidays/descriptive language

**1** Choose the correct word in *italics*.

1 For a good holiday, I like lying on a *rock/sandy/sand* beach.

2 I was impressed by the lovely *scene/scenery/scenic* in Morocco's Atlas Mountains.

3 I was so tired. I slept the sleep of the *dead/die/death*.

4 We sat by the river and watched the *going down/moving/setting* sun. The sky was filled with reds and oranges.

5 Have you ever heard the sound of a *lion/dog/mouse* roaring?

6 In the market, this really cool T-shirt caught my *seeing/sight/eye*. I had to buy it.

7 Prague is one of Europe's great *sensation/historic/history* capitals.

8 We had a truly *forgetful/forgotten/unforgettable* journey around Russia.

## Grammar | Past Perfect Simple

**2** <u>Underline</u> examples of the Past Perfect in the sentences below.

1 He had forgotten his camera.

2 It was the most beautiful place we had ever seen.

3 We had never expected such silence from a place so large.

4 Jack had been to Mexico before.

5 I'd seen it on TV loads of times.

**3** Read the story. Write the answers to the questions using the phrases in the box and the verbs in the Past Perfect form.

> come a day early
> forget to bring his passport
> leave his windows open
> not reserve accommodation
> win enough money for a great holiday

1 Why did Jimmie decide to go round the world?

2 What made Jimmie go back home from the airport?

3 What did he realise when he got back home?

4 Why did he have a list of hotels in his pocket?

5 Why did Jimmie laugh?

## How to ... | describe a memorable photo

**4** Read what Chee Yun says about her holiday photos. Complete the sentences with the words from the box.

> afterwards   been   excited   foreground   one
> right   shows

This photo (1)_____ the Iguazu Falls. The Falls are on the border of Brazil, Paraguay and Argentina. You can see the two guys we met on the (2)_____ .

After winning some money on the lottery, Jimmie decided to go on the holiday of a lifetime and travel round the world. When he got to the airport, he realised his passport was still at home. So he had to go back and get it. When he arrived back home again, he noticed that his windows were still open. He was so forgetful sometimes! So he shut them, and went back to the airport. His first stop was New York. He didn't have a hotel reservation, but he had the phone numbers and addresses of some hotels in his pocket, so he could find a hotel when he arrived. Back at the airport, he showed his ticket and passport to the clerk. But the clerk said 'I'm sorry, sir. It's the wrong day. Your flight is tomorrow.' Jimmie just laughed.

This (3)_____ is of the carnival in Recifé. You can see the floats, those big open buses full of people in costumes, in the (4)_____ .

I love this photo. We were really (5)_____ because we were on Sugar Loaf Mountain in Rio for the first time. We had (6)_____ on the chairlift, it was fantastic! (7)_____ , we went for a big meal in a restaurant.

## Listening

**5** Match the phrase beginnings (1–5) with the phrase endings (a–e).

1 wild    a attacked
2 luxury    b animals
3 be    c food
4 greatest    d flights
5 cheap    e challenge

**6** **a** You will listen to an interview with a travel journalist called Melissa. Which of the following do you think Melissa will talk about?

a her favourite trip ☐
b advice for people who want to be travel writers ☐
c equipment she uses ☐
d how tourism has changed ☐
e how long she has been a travel writer ☐

**b** 🔵 18 Cover the audioscript. Listen and tick the things from exercise 6a that Melissa mentions.

**c** Listen again and answer the questions.

1 How does Melissa feel about her travels?
2 When did she become a travel writer?
3 What is the 'good thing' about modern travel?
4 How has climbing Mount Everest changed?
5 Why does she mention Sandy Hill Pitman?
6 What two pieces of advice does she give to young travel writers?

### AUDIOSCRIPT

**I:** Melissa, you've travelled to and written about over sixty countries, and seen some amazing things. But in a recent interview you say that your journey has only just begun.

**M:** I feel that way, yes. I think, as you see more, you realise there's more to see. You visit one country, then you want to go and see its neighbours. So, yes, I do feel I'm just starting.

**I:** How many years have you been a travel writer?

**M:** A long time, more than thirty years.

**I:** What changes have you seen in travel and tourism?

**M:** Well, many. I think these new airlines that offer cheap flights all over the world have made a big difference. People – not necessarily rich people – can now see more of the world, and I think that's a good thing.

**I:** And there's a bad side too?

**M:** Of course. I think, well, just as an example: Mount Everest. Mount Everest used to be probably the greatest challenge for any traveller. Well, now it's full of tourists. Tour guides can take you up the mountain and you don't need any training because the guides do everything for you. There was the case of Sandy Hill Pitman in 1996. Her guides carried her laptop computer, coffee machine and luxury food up Everest. Now, for me, that's the bad side of modern tourism. You lose some of the mystery.

**I:** Melissa, is there any advice you would give to young people who want to be travel writers?

**M:** Yes, I think the first thing is that you have to make time to write. Wherever you are – in a desert, on a boat, at the top of a mountain. You have to find the time. And if you do it every day, it becomes a habit. The second thing is details. You must look for details. It's no good writing 'The sunset was beautiful'. You have to say exactly what colours you saw. How the sun felt on your face. You have to be very detailed and look more deeply than most people.

## Vocabulary | places in a city

**1**　**a** Find sixteen places to visit in a city in the wordsearch. The words can go across or down.

| L | I | E | A | I | O | R | Q | Q | I | E | T | R |
|---|---|---|---|---|---|---|---|---|---|---|---|---|
| L | L | D | W | L | I | B | R | A | R | Y | B | O |
| F | M | P | A | L | A | C | E | X | Z | A | C | U |
| H | I | A | H | C | A | F | E | M | I | K | A | N |
| O | Y | G | A | R | D | E | N | U | R | Z | S | D |
| F | O | U | N | T | A | I | N | S | G | H | T | A |
| V | S | Q | U | A | R | E | A | E | A | H | L | B |
| B | O | O | K | S | H | O | P | U | L | O | E | O |
| H | O | T | E | L | L | P | Q | M | L | S | K | U |
| C | A | N | A | L | A | A | S | H | E | T | A | T |
| A | L | U | M | X | K | R | X | I | R | E | Y | C |
| V | V | C | W | C | E | K | L | W | Y | L | J | T |
| G | Y | S | M | A | R | K | E | T | X | X | A | T |

**b** Which two places might you visit …

1 to stay the night? _____ and _____
2 to see paintings and sculptures? _____ and _____
3 to buy things? _____ and _____
4 to see water? _____ and _____
5 to go inside an old building? _____ and _____

## How to... | get around a new place

**2**　**a** Match the question beginnings and endings.

1 Excuse me, is there
2 Do you know where
3 How much is a
4 What time does the hostel
5 Could you tell me the way

a) to the Wawel Castle, please?
b) single to the city centre?
c) a good cheap restaurant nearby?
d) the station is, please?
e) close at night?

**b** Match the answers (a–e) with the questions (1–5) in exercise 2a.

a 2 euros.
b Yes, there's an excellent Chinese place just round the corner.
c That depends. Do you mean the bus station or the railway station?
d Just go straight on, and it's on your right.
e The doors are locked at 10:30.

## Pronunciation | intonation in questions

**3**　**a** Put the words in the correct order to make questions.

1 What/is/it?/time
2 this/Who/is/a/of?/picture
3 Is/here?/chemist/there/a/near
4 station/is?/Do/know/where/you/the
5 much/does/How/the/tour/cost?/sightseeing
6 you/tell/the/art/gallery?/me/the/way/to/Could
7 ever/Have/you/been/holiday?/a/camping/on

**b** Which questions in exercise 3a are …

a *Wh-* questions (*e.g What time does the museum close?*)?
b Indirect questions (*Could you tell me what time the train leaves?*)?
c Yes/No questions (*Is there a bank near here?*)?

**c** Practise saying the questions using the correct intonation patterns.

**d** 🔘 19 Listen and check.

## Grammar | uses of *like*

**4** Correct the mistakes in the sentences.

1 How's the flat like? Is it big?
2 Do you like some help? I'm free at the moment.
3 Your house is look like a museum. I love your old furniture.
4 I like listen to music. My favourite band is The White Stripes.
5 What is your girlfriend look like? Is she tall and blonde? I think I saw her yesterday.
6 What's that film likes? I've heard it's very sad.
7 What would you like do this evening? There's a good film on at the cinema.
8 What did the weather like? I hope it didn't rain and ruin your holiday.

# Reading

**5 a** Read the article. Match the places (a–f) with the paragraphs (1–5). There are two places in one of the paragraphs.

a Roswell, USA
b Papua New Guinea
c Dubai, UAE
d Sahara Desert
e Lajamanu, Australia
f Bhutan

**b** Match the headings (a–e) with the paragraphs (1–5).

a Where can I see some crazy weather?
b Where can I watch sharks safely?
c Where can I learn about UFOs?
d Where can I find some peace and quiet?
e Where can I meet remote tribes?

**c** What do these numbers refer to in the article?

9,065,000 *the size of the Sahara Desert (in square kilometres)*

1 11
2 10,000,000
3 500
4 8,000

**d** Read the article again. Mark the sentences true (T) or false (F).

1 You need to swim underwater to watch the sharks.
2 Visitors to Roswell will see little green men.
3 People go fishing in the river at Lajamanu.
4 It is easier to go to the Sahara than to Bhutan.
5 Kelly Woolford is a tourist in Papua New Guinea.

# Amazing experiences in amazing places

**1 ____**
If you're in the United Arab Emirates, why not go to the Dubai Aquarium? Every day at 4:00 p.m., divers get into the 10-million litre fish tank, and feed the sharks. And you can watch from 11 metres below the surface. But don't worry — you don't need to get wet. Just walk down the aquarium tunnel for an unforgettable view!

**2 ____**
Go to the International UFO Museum and Research Center, in Roswell, USA. Something strange fell out of the sky in 1947, and people have been going there ever since. Don't expect to see any little green men, though: there aren't any!

**3 ____**
Talking of strange things falling out of the sky, one day in 2010 in Lajamanu, Australia, it rained fish. Yes, hundreds of fish fell from the sky into the town. The amazing thing is that the nearest river is 500 km away. So how did it happen? Winds in a thunderstorm lifted the fish out of the water and took them as far as Lajamanu. Believe it or not, this happens quite often in Lajamanu!

**4 ____**
Go to Bhutan in the Himalayas. There are very few cars, so wherever you go, it's very calm and peaceful. Going to Bhutan is like traveling back in time. The only problem is getting into the country, as visas are limited. Still, if you can't get one, go to the Sahara Desert. It's 9,065,000 square kilometres, so there should be enough space for everybody!

**5 ____**
Go to Papua New Guinea. Kelly Woolford of First Contact holidays will take you on a three-week trip for $8,000. There, you will trek through the rainforest and search out traditional tribespeople. Kelly Woolford says, 'There are places in West Papua which are untouched (by modern travellers). People are too scared to go there.'

## Vocabulary | travelling

**1** **a** Complete the sentences with words from the box.

> barren   camping   local   package   sandy
> tropical

1 I just want to find a nice _____ beach, where I can sunbathe all day.

2 If you want to visit a _____ rainforest, then go to the Amazon.

3 My parents took us on several _____ holidays when we were children. We arranged everything ourselves and stayed in campsites.

4 The best thing about a _____ holiday is that everything is arranged for you.

5 Is the Sahara just a _____ desert, with no plants or anything?

6 Don't you think the best way to experience _____ culture is to go to a market?

**b** Write the phrases from exercise 1a which match these definitions.

a sandy place without any water or wildlife.
*barren desert*

1 a trip where you buy one ticket for your transport and accommodation. _____

2 a hot wet place with lots of wildlife. _____

3 the way people in a particular place behave and live. _____

4 a nice place by the sea. _____

## Pronunciation | sentence stress

**2** **a** Read the dialogues aloud. Underline the words which speaker B stresses most.

1 A: Are you a tea or coffee drinker?
   B: I hate coffee, but I love tea.

2 A: Did you like the book or the film more?
   B: The book was great, but the film is rubbish.

3 A: Where did you stay when you were in Paris?
   B: We couldn't afford a hotel, so we just stayed in a hostel.

4 A: Do you read a lot then?
   B: Yeah, but I don't waste money in expensive bookshops. I just borrow things from libraries.

5 A: Here's your meal, sir.
   B: Oh, I asked for chicken and rice, but you've brought me chicken and chips.

**b** 🔊 20 Listen to check.

## Grammar | articles

**3** Complete the website with *a*, *the* or – (no article).

## Bill's Geography website

**– for the lost and confused! Send in your questions!**

### Today's Questions and Answers

1 **Q:** Is Northern Ireland part of *a/–/the* UK?
   **A:** Yes, but *a/–/the* Republic of Ireland is a separate country.

2 **Q:** Is *a/–/the* Russia in Europe or Asia?
   **A:** It's in both. Parts of *a/–/the* country are in Asia and other parts are in Europe.

3 **Q:** Where and what are *a/–/the* Andes?
   **A:** It's *a/–/the* mountain range that runs through several countries in South America.

4 **Q:** What is *a/–/the* sunniest place on earth?
   **A:** *a/–/the* Sahara Desert. The sun shines virtually all day, every day: ninety-seven percent of the time.

5 **Q:** Can you tell me about *a/–/the* Monaco?
   **A:** It's *a/–/the* principality in Europe. It's small and rich.

6 **Q:** Is *a/–/the* Nile in Africa?
   **A:** Yes, it's *a/–/the* longest river on that continent.

7 **Q:** Can you tell me something about *a/–/the* Nauru? I think it's a country.
   **A:** It's *a/–/the* tiny island in the Pacific Ocean, and you're right – it is a country.

8 **Q:** Is it true that no one lives in *a/–/the* Greenland?
   **A:** No! But it is *a/–/the* coldest island in the world. eighty-five percent of Greenland is covered in ice.

# Reading

**4** **a** What do travel agents do? Choose from the options below.

1  book flights for people ☐
2  tell customers what documents they need ☐
3  help customers get the plane seat that they want ☐
4  find cheap holidays ☐
5  help customers rent cars for their trip ☐
6  tell people which plane to get on ☐

**b** Read the stories. Tick (✓) the things from exercise 4a that are mentioned.

**c** Read the stories again. Mark the sentences true (T) or false (F).

1  It takes less than one hour to get from Detroit to Chicago. ☐
2  One man was looking for his flight number on the aeroplanes. ☐
3  A customer wanted to drive from Heathrow Airport to Namibia. ☐
4  A woman didn't want to sit near a window because of her hair. ☐
5  A businessman was going to Colombia for the first time. ☐
6  One customer wanted to smoke on the plane. ☐

**d** What are the definitions of the words? Choose a or b.

1  *Time zone* means
   a  an area where the clocks are set at a particular time.
   b  a place where you go if you are late.
2  *Stopover* means
   a  the place where you finish the journey.
   b  a scheduled stop on a journey, before starting again.
3  An *aisle* seat in a plane is
   a  a seat next to the corridor (not close to the window).
   b  a seat next to the window.
4  *Travel documents* means
   a  a film about a holiday destination.
   b  official papers you need when you travel.
5  A *long haul* flight means
   a  a very large aeroplane.
   b  a flight from one continent to another.

# Travel Agents' True Stories

We asked travel agents to write in and tell us about their funniest moments. Here are some of the stories.

I had a client once who called from the airport, saying, 'How do I know which plane to get on?' I asked him what he meant and he said, 'I was told my plane was flight 554, but none of these planes have numbers on them.'

A woman phoned me from Detroit. She wanted to know how it was possible that her flight from Detroit left at 8:20 a.m. and arrived in Chicago at 8:33 a.m. I explained that Chicago was an hour ahead of Detroit, but she didn't understand the idea of time zones. Eventually, I just told her the plane was very fast. She was happy with that.

A man who was travelling to Namibia via London's Heathrow Airport asked if he could rent a car at Heathrow. I noticed that he only had a one-hour stopover in Heathrow Airport, so I asked him why he wanted to rent a car. He said he'd heard that the airport was really big, so he needed a car to drive to his next flight.

One customer was booking a seat on a plane. She asked for an aisle seat so that her hair wouldn't get messed up by being near the window.

A businessman called me about travel documents for Colombia. I told him he needed a passport and visa. He said he didn't need a visa. I checked again and I was definitely right. I called back to explain that he needed it, and he said, 'The last time I was there I didn't need a Visa. They took American Express.'

I booked a customer on a long haul flight from Oslo to Mexico. He asked if it was a non-smoking flight, and I told him it was. He asked if it would be OK to smoke on the plane if he opened the window.

# Vocabulary | expressions with *get*

**5** Write an expression with *get* to replace the words in *italics* in the sentences. Make sure you use the correct verb tense.

1  They decided *to have their wedding* in Florida. _____
2  I really think my English *is improving*. _____
3  We're *returning* before 5:00. _____
4  He's always *had a great relationship* with his mother-in-law. _____
5  I usually *put on my clothes* at about 8:00 in the morning. _____
6  She wanted to go home, but she *couldn't find the way*. _____

## Past Perfect Simple and Past Simple

**1** Choose the best follow-up to the first sentences, a or b.

1 She was amazed when she saw Chartres Cathedral.
   a She had never seen anything so beautiful.
   b She never saw anything so beautiful.

2 There were crowds of tourists standing around the Mona Lisa. It was amazing –
   a we expected so many people.
   b we hadn't expected so many people.

3 The land stretching out in front of us was completely dry.
   a It had rained for months.
   b It hadn't rained for months.

4 Watching India pass by through the train window, I relaxed and finally
   a enjoyed the view.
   b had enjoyed the view.

5 Suddenly Janine appeared at my front door. I was shocked.
   a Why had she called first?
   b Why hadn't she called first?

6 Poland is one of the most interesting countries I've ever been to.
   a I'd been there last August.
   b I went there last August.

7 I had always wanted to visit the temples at Bagan in Burma, and
   a I finally went there last year.
   b I had finally been there last year.

8 The hotel looked great, but they couldn't give us a room because
   a we booked.
   b we hadn't booked.

9 The weather was so disappointing during my holiday.
   a I had hoped to spend a few days on the beach, but it was impossible.
   b I hoped to spend a few days on the beach but it was impossible.

10 Poland is one of the most interesting countries I've ever been to.
   a I'd gone there last August.
   b I went there last August.

## Past Perfect Simple, Past Simple and articles

**2** Complete the sentences with *a*, *the* or – (no article) and the Past Perfect Simple or the Past Simple form of the verbs in brackets.

1 She was sad because she found out that she _____ (fail) _____ final law exam.

2 I wanted to become _____ nurse. But in the end I _____ (become) a doctor.

3 I arrived at _____ party at 8:00 but I _____ (not/stay) long. What about you?

4 He got hurt during judo. Later they discovered that he _____ (break) _____ his leg.

5 _____ computers _____ (start) to become popular with the public in the 1990s.

6 When they returned, _____ children _____ (already/fall) asleep.

7 That afternoon I told the police that I _____ (not/recognise) _____ burglar's face.

8 I'm sure we can find _____ good café. There were lots when I _____ (come) here in 2008.

9 It seemed like _____ interesting programme. I _____ (never/see) it before.

10 _____ lions tend to sleep during the day. When I _____ (go) to Africa, I saw a few.

## Uses of *like*

**3** Complete the sentences with *like*. Add any further necessary words.

Tell me about Warsaw.
What's *it like*?

1 Do they want some milk?
   Would _____ ?

2 I'm not interested in being famous.
   I wouldn't _____ .

3 Tell me about Johnny's appearance when you last saw him.
   What did _____ ?

4 It tastes the same as meat.
   It _____ .

5 Can you describe robots of the future?
   What will _____ ?

6 I've never been keen on rock music.
   I've never _____ .

7 Is Spanish grammar similar to Portuguese grammar?
   Is _____ ?

8 Luisa and her sister, Daniela, look the same.
   Luisa _____ .

9 Mum, how was life in the 1960s?
   Mum, what _____ ?

## Articles

**4  a** Two of these sentences are correct. Add an article where necessary to the other six sentences.

1  It's small, pretty town in the south of England, famous for cider, a drink made with apples.
2  They're tall and handsome, and oldest one has a really good sense of humour.
3  No! I think it's the most disgusting food I've ever eaten!
4  Horses. I wanted to be horse trainer when I was younger.
5  It was a brilliant place, and owner was very friendly.
6  My mother, I think. We have similar noses.
7  It's one of the biggest buildings in city, and it's made of glass.
8  Yes, please. Actually, can I have piece of toast?

**b** Match the sentences (1–8) in exercise 4a with the questions (a–h).

a  Would you like some bread with your soup?
b  What does the Modern Art Gallery look like?
c  What's Taunton like?
d  Who do you look like in your family?
e  What was that restaurant like before it closed down?
f  Do you like that Scottish dish, haggis?
g  What type of animals do you like?
h  What are your cousins like?

## Vocabulary

**5** Choose the correct word in *italics*.

1  I went on a *travel/tour* around Venice last summer.
2  I love the view of *snowing/snowcapped* mountains.
3  There's a *sightseeing/sightsee* tour tomorrow – shall we go?
4  It's a very *scenery/scenic* place.
5  The resort has a great *sandy/sand* beach, that's really quiet too.
6  The *lake/fountain* is switched off every night.
7  In the centre of the city, there's a lovely old *square/roundabout*, where you can sit and enjoy a drink.
8  Most university students stay in the big student *hostel/hotel* behind the train station.

**6** Match the expressions with *get* in *italics* in the sentences (1–6) with the meanings (a–f).

1  When will we *get to* the airport?
2  I was learning the game, but I *got bored*.
3  Nearly fifty percent of married couples *get divorced* after ten years or less.
4  I'll *get* you a drink later.
5  Can you come and *get me* from the station?
6  It takes a long time to really *get to know* the geography of London.

a  arrive at
b  buy
c  end their marriages
d  lost interest and stopped
e  pick me up
f  learn

## How to …

**7** Add a word to each line said by **A** to correct the mistakes.

1  **A:** Excuse me. Is there post office near here?
   **B:** There's one on your left.
2  **A:** Can you tell me way to the theatre, please?
   **B:** Yes. Go straight on. It's right in front of you.
3  **A:** What time the museum close?
   **B:** At 6:30.
4  **A:** How is a ticket to the city centre?
   **B:** €3.20.
5  **A:** Excuse me. Could you tell me to get to Eve's Restaurant?
   **B:** Eve's Restaurant? Sorry, I don't know it.
6  **A:** Does this train go the airport?
   **B:** Yes, it does.
7  **A:** Do you know much a hire car costs per day?
   **B:** It's about £20, not including insurance.
8  **A:** Can recommend a good nightclub?
   **B:** Yes. Splash Deever is good if you like hip-hop.
9  **A:** This is a photo took when I was on holiday last year.
   **B:** Oh, I see. You're a good photographer.
10 **A:** Who's the lady the left?
   **B:** That's my mum.

## Vocabulary | learning

**1** Choose the correct words in *italics*.

1 I started playing the trumpet last year, but I haven't *made/done/had* a lot of progress. It still sounds terrible!

2 I'm *making/doing/getting* a Spanish course at the moment.

3 I *made/got/did* Law at university.

4 I drank a lot of coffee while I was *passing/failing/revising* for my exams.

5 When I graduated *to/from/at* university, I started looking for a job.

6 I tend to *make/do/take* my research on the Internet.

7 I didn't *make/got/get* good marks in my exams.

8 Did you *take/do/go* notes during the lecture?

9 **A:** Are you coming with us for lunch?
   **B:** No. I'm just *having/going/doing* to my class.

10 I've *got/made/graduated* a degree in English Literature from London University.

11 My father *graduated/passed/revised* from the same university as me.

12 Great news! I *made/went/passed* the exam – and I got 99 percent!

**2** Complete the dialogues with suitable words.

1 **A:** In this job you need to learn things very quickly.
   **B:** Yes, you are _____ in at the deep end.

2 **A:** I'm not very good at this yet.
   **B:** Keep trying. Practice makes _____.

3 **A:** How are your driving lessons going?
   **B:** OK, but it's such a steep _____ curve. There's so much to learn!

4 **A:** That's a lovely poem!
   **B:** Yes, I learnt it by _____ when I was at school.

5 **A:** How is your German?
   **B:** Not very good. I _____ a lot of mistakes.

6 **A:** How did you learn to use this programme so quickly?
   **B:** I took a crash _____ in it, and after one day I knew enough to use it.

## How to... | describe a learning experience

**3** Complete the text with the prepositions.

> for (x2)   in (x2)   of (x2)   up

When I was seventeen, I took an interest (1) _____ juggling. I was studying (2) _____ my university entrance exams at the time, so perhaps it wasn't the best time to start a new hobby! I needed to revise (3) _____ my school biology exams AND learn the basics (4) _____ medicine. I spent hours at my desk, but sometimes it got so boring! So a friend and I took a crash course (5) _____ juggling just for a laugh, and I picked it (6) _____ quite fast. I'd practise over and over. My mum always told me it was a complete waste (7) _____ time, and that I should be studying. But I actually found it really useful – after five minutes juggling, I felt relaxed and ready to get back to work.

## Grammar | subject/object questions

**4** **a** Put the words in the correct order to make questions.

1 the/Cup/held/World/Which/2010?/country/in

2 Who/American/election/2008?/won/the/in

3 Florence?/the/created/Who/David/in/statue/of

4 city/What/Pompeii?/of/destroyed/the

5 the/Where/Parliament?/is/European

6 Which/nearly/islands?/country/180,000/has

7 language/What/do/speak/in/they/Brazil?

8 did/When/the/come/Berlin/Wall/down?

**b** Match the questions (1–8) in exercise 4a with the answers (a–h).

a In 1989.

b A volcano.

c In Brussels.

d Portuguese.

e Barack Obama.

f South Africa.

g Michelangelo.

h Finland.

**5** Correct the mistakes in five of the questions.

1 Who did give Mina my email address?
2 When did you get back from holiday?
3 Who the book belongs to?
4 Who did invented the computer?
5 Who invited Matthew to the party?
6 Which train did they catch?
7 Where lives Marianna?
8 What did happened at the meeting?

## Reading

**6** The sentences (a–d) have been taken out of the article below. Read the article and complete the gaps (1–4) with the sentences.

a They fail to see them as part of the learning process.
b Learn to talk about your mistakes, at work and at home.
c Then they restart the computer, and experiment again.
d People who achieve great success then have more to lose when things go wrong.

**7** What do the words in **bold** in the article refer to?

Line 2: **it** *making mistakes*

1 Line 8: them _____
2 Line 18: they _____
3 Line 25: this _____
4 Line 29: this _____

**8** Find words or expressions in the article which mean ...

1 make you annoyed _____ (line 3)
2 falling on the ground _____ (line 4)
3 saying something with the wrong pronunciation _____ (line 5)
4 throw and catch three or more balls together _____ (line 6)
5 a button on a computer _____ (line 16)
6 do something in a way that people don't expect _____ (4 words) (line 24)
7 do things that could cause problems _____ (line 28)
8 possibilities for things you can do _____ (line 30)

## Learning from mistakes

Have you ever noticed how children are always making mistakes? They do **it** all the time, and it doesn't seem to bother them. You don't learn to walk without falling over. You don't learn to speak without
5 mispronouncing lots of words. You don't learn to juggle without dropping balls. But if you create an environment where mistakes are not accepted, then people become frightened of **them**.

**(1)** _____ . In these kinds of environments people
10 learn to hide their mistakes, and not to celebrate them as a good thing. If you're not making mistakes then you're not learning anything valuable.

It's interesting to see what happens when someone uses a computer for the first time. When an older
15 person starts using a computer, they are often worried about pressing the wrong key. Perhaps they are worried about deleting files by mistake. But children aren't like that. **They** experiment with all the buttons, just to see what will happen. **(2)** _____ .
20 And they are learning from every move they make. The fear of failure seems to develop as we go through school. We learn to become afraid of our mistakes, to be afraid of having the wrong answer, or to draw outside the lines.

25 The fear of success comes later, and we can see **this** often in successful professionals and leaders. **(3)** _____ . So they start to worry, and decide not to take risks.

Don't let **this** happen to you. **(4)** _____ . See what
30 opportunities can arise from the mistakes you make, and soon you'll feel happier about yourself.

## Vocabulary | personal qualities

**1** Match the adjectives from the box with the sentences.

> boring   encouraging   inspiring
> ~~knowledgeable~~   patient   understanding

He knows so much about so many things. *He's very knowledgeable.*

1 He always tells you that you're doing well. _____

2 His books are wonderful. They give me lots of ideas. _____

3 She can always deal with difficult situations without getting angry. _____

4 He talks too slowly, and doesn't say anything interesting. _____

5 You can talk to her about your problems, and she knows how you're feeling. _____

## Vocabulary | word building (1)

**2** Replace the word in brackets with the correct part of speech (verb, adjective or noun).

He's very (~~imagination~~) *imaginative*, and has lots of creative ideas.

1 I really hate the feeling of (boring) _____ .

2 Can you please (clarity) _____ one thing: what am I supposed to do?

3 You need to be more (tolerate) _____ when people don't agree with you.

4 I don't know why, but spiders really (fright) _____ me.

5 He's very (know) _____ about his country's history and customs.

6 Having (patient) _____ with children when they are learning new things is very important.

## Pronunciation | word stress in word building

**3** **a** Look at the picture. What is the woman trying to do? Read the text to check your ideas.

I want to **encourage** my son to think about the job he's going to do when he's older. I want him to have an **interesting** job. But it's **frightening** to think that, if he makes the wrong **decision** now, he might spend his life doing a job he hates. He really loves **electric** things, so maybe he'll be a great **scientist**. But he's also very **artistic**, so maybe he'll become a great painter or **musician**. Still, there's plenty of time for us to decide how we're going to **educate** him. He hasn't even learned to walk yet!

**b** Put the words in **bold** in exercise 3a in the correct column (A or B) according to their stress.

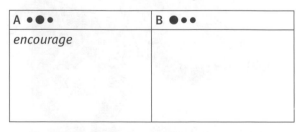

| A ●●● | B ●●● |
|-------|-------|
| *encourage* | |
| | |
| | |
| | |

**c** 🌐 21 Now listen and check. There should be five words in the first column and four in the second.

## Grammar | *used to* and *would*

**4** Replace the Past Simple with *used to/would* in the sentences, where possible.

*When I was a child ...*

1 *I spent my holidays with my grandparents.*
2 *My grandmother cooked delicious meals.*
3 *She kept chickens, goats and horses.*
4 *My cousin and I rode the horses every day.*
5 *My favourite horse was called Racer.*
6 *Racer was faster than all the other horses.*
7 *I didn't understand how dangerous riding could be.*
8 *One day I fell off Racer and broke my arm.*
9 *My mother didn't let me ride him again.*
10 *After that, I sat in the house and watched sadly as the horses played in the field.*

**5** **a** Rewrite the sentences using *used to*.

1 I played volleyball when I was at school. I don't play now.
2 Sylvie doesn't smoke now. Did she smoke before?
3 When I was younger, I didn't like mushrooms. I love them now.
4 I enjoyed cooking a lot before. Now I don't have enough time.
5 She drank milk when she was a child but now she is allergic to it.
6 He didn't play computer games before. Now he is always playing them.
7 I read a lot of books when I was at university. I don't read so many now.
8 You don't study there now, but did you go to the Anglo-American School before?

## Listening

**6**  22 Cover the audioscript. Listen to the description of a young boy called Roger starting school. Then answer the questions.

1 Before Roger started school, how did he feel about going to school?
2 When he started school, what did he think was the most important thing to learn?
3 How do you think Roger felt about Miss Bradshaw and the headteacher?

**7** **a** Read the story again. Mark the sentences true (T) or false (F).

1 Roger thought he would never grow up. ☐
2 His mother never talked to him about school. ☐
3 Roger was very happy about his first day at school. ☐
4 Roger was put in a class with the big children. ☐
5 He thought the most important thing to do at school was not to move. ☐
6 Roger was punished at school. ☐
7 He thought that if he moved he would get a reward. ☐
8 In his classroom he practised learning numbers and letters. ☐
9 The headteacher asked if Roger was a naughty boy. ☐
10 Miss Bradshaw said that Roger's behaviour was better. ☐

**b** 22 Listen to check.

### AUDIOSCRIPT

I was born on 4 November 1956. I think I always thought that I would spend my whole life just being a child, and living at home with my parents. Sometimes my mother would mention something called 'school', but she always said that I didn't need to worry. I didn't understand this, as whatever 'school' was, I didn't plan to go there. Then, one morning, she woke me up early and said, 'Today you go to school, Roger.' I was terrified, and thought to myself, 'This is the end of my life.'

That first day at Elementary School I quickly came to understand the most important thing about education – it was all about keeping still. As I entered the hall, a large hand took me away from my mother, and put me in a line with some other small children. And then a loud voice commanded 'KEEP STILL!' I stood very, very still, thinking that if I even moved one small part of my body, I would get some terrible punishment. I checked my body – feet and legs – keeping still, body and arms – keeping still, head and eyes – oh no – what about my eyes? Were they moving?

Inside the classroom, there were the same rules. I was put behind a desk and all I can remember was this tall, thin lady – Miss Bradshaw, our teacher – who kept shouting at us to 'Keep still!' while she was talking. 'How can I write and keep still?' I thought. 'Can I open my book?' After a month the situation was the same, and instead of concentrating on unimportant things like learning numbers and letters, I spent all my time practising very hard the art of keeping still.

I was rewarded, as one day the headteacher came into the classroom. 'Stand up for the Headmistress!' shouted Miss Bradshaw. 'Who are the naughty children?' asked the headteacher. 'What about you, Roger?' I stood very still and tried to look serious. Miss Bradshaw replied, 'No, not any more. Roger is much less trouble than he used to be,' and I smiled a long, warm smile.

## Subject and object questions

**1** Correct the mistakes in six of the questions.

1 Who did go to the meeting?
2 Which room did they go to?
3 What did happen?
4 Where did was Shakespeare born?
5 Who did write *The Castle*?
6 Which character did you like best?
7 Who did telephone the engineer?
8 What did he say?
9 When did you see her?
10 Who did eat the cake?

## *used to* and *would*/Past Simple

**2** Tick (✓) the correct options, a, b or c. There may be more than one correct option.

1 When I was a boy I _____ a bicycle.
   a use to ride ☐
   b used to ride ☐
   c would rode ☐

2 As a young girl she _____ .
   a always loving paint ☐
   b always loved painting ☐
   c would always love painting ☐

3 We _____ in a huge house in the countryside.
   a would live ☐
   b used to live ☐
   c lived ☐

4 My grandfather _____ me how to cook.
   a would show ☐
   b showed ☐
   c use to show ☐

5 I didn't _____ listening to opera music.
   a use to enjoy ☐
   b enjoyed ☐
   c would enjoy ☐

6 He once _____ me he would never leave.
   a used to promise ☐
   b would promise ☐
   c promised ☐

7 As children we _____ very naughty.
   a were ☐
   b used to being ☐
   c would be ☐

8 Yesterday, I _____ to the cinema.
   a used to go ☐
   b went ☐
   c would go ☐

## Modals of ability, past and present

**3** Choose the correct words in *italics*.

1 Ivan *could/managed/was able to* to get us some tickets for the show.
2 We *managed not to/couldn't/didn't able* see properly because we were in the back row.
3 Were you *able/manage/could* to read my handwriting?
4 I didn't *could/manage/able* to send him a message in time.
5 Problems meant that they *couldn't/didn't manage/weren't able* finish the job.
6 Did you *manage to/able to/could* get her autograph?
7 I *didn't manage/couldn't/wasn't able* swim until I was 22.
8 She *couldn't/wasn't able* to understand my accent.
9 I *was able/could/managed* speak three languages before I was six years old.
10 We *didn't manage/able/couldn't* contact you immediately.

## Lifelong learning (using a correction code)

**4** Correct the mistakes using the correction code from unit 7.

I decided to brush out [*WW – up*] on my German before my holiday to germany [1 _____], and enrolled on an intensive course at my college local [2 _____]. It was a pretty steap [3 _____] learning curve, and I was amazed how much I'd forgotten from [4 _____] my at school time [5 _____]. In those days, I've been [6 _____] quite good, and I knew the grammar inside out.

At [7 _____] end of the corse [8 _____] there had been [9 _____] a test. It was all multiple choice. When I didn't know [10 _____] answer, I just made a wild guessing [11 _____]. Well, I must be the world's best guesser, because somehow I passed with fly [12 _____] colours. I've no idea how I did it? [13 _____]

# Vocabulary

5 Use the clues to complete the crossword.

## Across

3 She g_____ last year from university with an Honours degree in Economics.

4 They say that practice makes p_____ .

7 She's such a b_____ – she's always reading!

9 He's the teacher's p _____. That's why he always gets good marks.

10 I'm not very good yet, but I'm making p_____ .

11 Unfortunately, you f_____ the exam.

13 Did you get good m_____ in your exam?

14 At university, I was late for all of my l_____ .

15 Have you r_____ for the history test?

## Down

1 It was hard work, and I was thrown in at the _____ end. I had to learn it all myself.

2 Do you have c_____ assessment, or just an exam at the end of the course?

5 I'm doing an art c_____ in the evenings.

6 We've been doing some r_____ into why people eat fast food.

8 I think I've made a terrible m_____ .

12 His lectures are so memorable you don't need to take n_____ .

6 Complete the sentences with the words and phrases from the box.

> brought   curve   deep   fast learner   heart
> perfect   picked   practice   steep   strict
> thrown

1 I learn things quickly. I'm a _____ .

2 We couldn't mess around in her lessons. She was a very _____ teacher.

3 Just keep trying and you'll get better. _____ makes _____ .

4 I have learnt so much in the first week. It's a _____ learning _____ .

5 I can sing all the Beatles' songs from memory. I learnt them by _____ .

6 I didn't have Spanish lessons. I just _____ it up when I was there on holiday.

7 We didn't have any training. We were just _____ in at the _____ end.

8 When I was a child, my parents _____ me up to respect older people.

7 Replace the words in brackets with a suitable word to complete the sentences.

1 My uncle was very k_____ (he knew a lot) about the war.

2 I explained the problems and he was very u_____ (he knew how I felt).

3 My teacher was very s_____ (she told us what to do and what not to do), and I was a bit frightened of her.

4 A good teacher needs to be very p_____ (able to wait without getting angry).

5 Teachers should always c_____ (explain clearly) what they mean.

6 Thank you for giving me so much e_____ (help which made me feel better).

# How to...

8 Complete the sentences with the words in the box.

> interest   know   sounds   surprised   though
> wonder

1 I _____ if you could tell me about your previous job?

2 It was a great experience, even _____ it was hard work.

3 I really didn't _____ what to expect ...

4 That _____ interesting, tell me a bit more ...

5 What _____ me was ...

6 About a year ago, I took an _____ in ...

## Vocabulary | change

**1** Complete the sentences with suitable words.

1 If you use Internet banking, change your p_____ regularly.

2 If we all try to use less electricity, then we can reduce c_____ change.

3 He used to be a lawyer, but then he changed c_____ and became a professional artist instead.

4 I was planning to go out with friends tonight, but I've changed my m_____ , and I'm staying at home.

5 I hate talking about politics. Can we change the s_____?

6 Sometimes, if you're feeling bad, a change of h_____ can cheer you up!

## Grammar | Second Conditional

**2** Choose the correct word in *italics*.

1 I *'ll/would* call you tomorrow if I hear from them.

2 If there were more police, there *won't/wouldn't* be so much crime.

3 If she *stops/stopped* smoking, she'll probably put on weight.

4 Where would you go if you *have/had* a free weekend?

5 If I had some more money, I *will/would* buy that coat.

6 Would it be a problem if I *will ask/asked* you for some help?

7 The house *is/would be* much cleaner if you helped.

8 We *wouldn't/won't* be here for long, if Eve gets her new job.

**3** Match the sentence beginnings (1–8) with the sentence endings (a–h) to make First or Second Conditional sentences.

1 If we have children

2 I'll earn lots of money

3 If Simon didn't spend all his money

4 If my computer crashes one more time

5 He won't watch so much TV

6 What would you say

7 If you had more cash

8 We'll spend more time outside

a I think I'll scream!

b would you buy a better mp3 player?

c when we move to a hot country.

d we'll need a bigger house.

e he could afford to buy a new car.

f if my blog becomes popular.

g if he asked you to marry him?

h if he starts going out in the evenings.

## Vocabulary | cities

**4** Put the letters in brackets in the correct order to make words to complete the blog.

I used to live in a tower (ckbol) *block* in one of the world's biggest cities. And I hated everything about the city. It was noisy because there was always (1 blngduii) _____ work everywhere. I lived a long way from my office, and because there was so much (2 cosgention) _____ , it took me over an hour to get to work during the (3 shru  hrou) _____ every morning and evening. I hated the sound of all those horns (4 hnoikng) _____ while angry drivers waited for the traffic lights to change. The smell of the (5 hauestx) _____ fumes from all those cars made me sick. So I decided to leave and move to the countryside, where it's really peaceful, and there are never any (6 citraff smaj) _____ . But you know what? Part of me still really misses the city.

## How to... | discuss problems and suggest changes

**5** **a** Read the text quickly. How many things would the writer like to change in his life?

> If I *could* change things in my life, what would I change?
>
> Well, there are certainly a things I'd like to change. I always seem to be in a hurry, so it be nice if I had more time. Life would be much better we had three-day weekends. And I suppose would like to live closer to my office. Actually no, it would better if I worked closer to my home. And I'd rather live in a palace than a flat, but there's not I can do about that. But apart that, I'm pretty happy with my life!

**b** Add one missing word to each sentence in the text.

> be ~~could~~ few from if much to would I

## Reading

**6** **a** Read the article. Match the pictures (A–D) with the paragraphs (1–6). Three paragraphs do not have pictures.

# Crazy laws

**1** It seems that the Greek philosopher, Aristotle, was right when he said, 'Even when laws have been written down, they ought not always to remain unaltered.' Laws in some parts of the world haven't changed for centuries, and some of them were strange right from the start!

**2** Did you know, for example, that London taxis (officially called Hackney carriages) are still legally required to carry hay and oats for their horses to eat? And in England, it is (1) _____ to stand within 100 yards (91 metres) of the Queen, without wearing socks? It is also illegal for a Member of Parliament to enter the Houses of Parliament, where these crazy laws are made and discussed, wearing a full suit of armour.

**3** If you live in Scotland, however, it's important to know that if someone knocks at the door of your house, and needs to use your toilet, you are legally required to let him in. But if you are Scottish you should stay away from the city of York, in the north of England. There, it is perfectly legal to shoot a Scotsman with a bow and arrow, unless it is a Sunday!

**4** But strange laws don't just exist in the UK. In France, you cannot call your pig Napoleon, and in Italy, a man can be (2) _____ for wearing a skirt. That's not all. In Alaska, US, while it's legal to shoot bears, waking a sleeping bear to take its photo is prohibited. Still in Alaska, it is considered an (3) _____ to push a live moose out of an aeroplane.

**5** Lots of the craziest laws seem to involve animals. In Hollywood, in the US it is illegal to take more than 2,000 sheep down Hollywood Boulevard at any one time. And in Florida, if an elephant is left tied to a parking meter, the parking fine must be paid, just as it would for a vehicle.

**6** Lastly, children are (4) _____ from going to school with their breath smelling of wild onions in West Virginia. And in Arkansas, teachers who have a certain haircut (a bob) will not be given a pay-rise. In Florida, a woman can be fined for falling asleep under the hair-dryer and unmarried women must not parachute on a Sunday. If they do, they might be arrested, receive a (5) _____ or be put in jail.

**b** Read the article again, then complete it with words from the box.

> arrested fine forbidden illegal offence

**c** Read the article again. Write true (T) or false (F).

1 Aristotle believed that laws should never change.
2 The UK has laws about what politicians are allowed to wear.
3 The French have laws about animal names.
4 People can take as many animals as they like down the streets of Hollywood.

# 8.3

## Grammar | Third Conditional

**1** Choose the correct options, a, b or c.

1 I _____ bought it if I'd known it was so difficult to use.

    **a** would have  **b** wouldn't have

    **c** wouldn't

2 We wouldn't have told him if we _____ how he would react.

    **a** had known  **b** knew  **c** had knew

3 If the tickets had been cheaper, there _____ more people at the show.

    **a** would been  **b** would have

    **c** would have been

4 They _____ the booking if they'd thought there were going to be so many people.

    **a** wouldn't cancelled

    **b** wouldn't have cancelled

    **c** haven't cancelled

5 He would have contacted us by now if the car _____ .

    **a** had arrived  **b** has arrived

    **c** had arrive

6 They would have told us if the flight _____ delayed.

    **a** has  **b** had be  **c** had been

7 I would have told you not to come if I _____ that the bank was closed.

    **a** realised  **b** had realised

    **c** have realised

8 The traffic was so bad it _____ quicker if we had walked.

    **a** was  **b** has been  **c** would have been

**2** **a** Match the sentences (1–6) with the picture stories (A–F).

1 They didn't have umbrellas, so they ended up getting wet.

2 There was water on the floor, so the waiter slipped and fell.

3 The man was able to buy the suit, because it was reduced by 90 percent.

4 Sam didn't know Tara had a boyfriend, so he invited her out to dinner.

5 They didn't know the restaurant was busy, so they didn't book a table.

6 Jane was stuck in heavy traffic, so arrived at the airport too late, and missed her plane.

**b** Write sentences about the picture stories in exercise 2a using the prompts and the verbs in brackets. Make sure you use the correct tense.

1 If there _____ (be) traffic, she _____ (miss) the plane.

2 If the suit _____ (be) reduced, the man _____ (be able) to buy it.

3 If there _____ (be) water on the floor, the waiter _____ (slip).

4 They _____ (get) so wet if they _____ (take) umbrellas.

5 If they _____ (realise) it would be so busy, they _____ (book) a table.

6 If he _____ (know) she had a boyfriend already, he _____ (invite) her out to dinner.

# Pronunciation | sentence stress in the Third Conditional

**3** **a** Look at the sentences from exercise 2b. Which words do you expect to be stressed?

**b** 🔘 25 Listen and check.

# Vocabulary | word building (2)

**4** Complete the words in the table with the prefixes and suffixes.

| -ence | in- | -ion | -ment | over- | un- |
|-------|-----|------|-------|-------|-----|

| | | |
|---|---|---|
| 1 | treat, move, punish, employ, arrange | _____ |
| 2 | _____ | expected, paid, surprisingly |
| 3 | independ, differ, intellig | _____ |
| 4 | _____ | dependent, human |
| 5 | congest, construct, direct | _____ |
| 6 | _____ | worked, cooked |

# Listening

**5** 🔘 26 Cover the audioscript. Listen to Rachel and Justin talking about decisions they have made and answer the questions for each person.

1 What was the decision about?

Rachel: _____

Justin: _____

2 What was the situation before?

Rachel: _____

Justin: _____

3 What was the situation afterwards?

Rachel: _____

Justin: _____

**6** Write *Rachel* or *Justin* for each statement.

1 _____ had always wanted to help people.

2 _____ wanted to be promoted.

3 _____ was unhappy at university.

4 _____ tries to finish work on time.

5 _____ had studied very hard at school.

6 _____ was often away from home.

**7** Listen again. Mark the sentences true (T) or false (F).

1 Rachel found it easy to decide what to do at university.

2 She had always wanted to be a psychologist.

3 Rachel was happy when she got a place at Medical School.

4 She enjoyed her university lectures.

5 Justin was a single man who enjoyed his freedom.

6 When he met Shan the things that were important to him changed.

7 Justin usually works late.

---

**AUDIOSCRIPT**

**Rachel:**

I think for me the most difficult decision I ever had to make was what to study at university. I started university studying medicine. I'd always wanted to be a doctor and to be able to help people. I'd studied very hard at school in order to pass the exams and get into Medical School. And I was delighted when I managed to. Then, surprisingly, when I started the course, I suddenly found that I wasn't happy with the decision. I didn't enjoy the lectures, and I found working in a hospital environment extremely difficult. I realised that I didn't want to spend the rest of my life doing this job after all. It was a very difficult decision at the time, but I left the university, and I ended up studying psychology instead. I don't regret the decision though. Not at all.

**Justin:**

I suppose deciding to buy a house and start a family was a big decision. Up until last year my work was the most important thing for me. I worked hard to try and get promoted, and I travelled a lot for business. In my free time, I went out with friends and generally had a lot of freedom. Then I met Shan, and we decided to live together, and my priorities started to change. We got married and started thinking about children. Now I try not to work late, and I've told my boss that I don't want to travel so much. I tend to spend my evenings at home babysitting, but I am happy with the decision. I think it is great to be able to spend time with your children when they are young.

# Review and consolidation unit 8

## First and Second Conditionals

**1** Choose the correct words in *italics*.

1 If we *wait/will wait/would wait* here, we'll see them when they arrive.

2 If I were you, I *won't/wouldn't/wasn't* go there.

3 If I *am going/went/would go* to university again, I would study sociology.

4 We'll stay in a beautiful hotel if we *go/went/would go* to Prague.

5 If you *gave/give/will give* him some money, he'd stop asking you.

6 She*'ll call/would call/called* us when she gets the message.

7 They wouldn't come unless they *will want/wanted/would want* to buy something.

8 She'd be so happy if she *won/win/would win* the race.

9 I *will/won't/didn't* know how to contact her unless she gets in touch.

10 You'll fail your exams if you *wouldn't start/didn't start/don't start* revising.

## Adverbs

**2** Choose the correct option, a, b or c.

1 She _____ packed her bags and left.
   a quickly
   b interestingly
   c completely

2 They _____ didn't want us to know about the money.
   a quickly
   b obviously
   c thoughtfully

3 She said the train arrived at 2:00, but it _____ doesn't get here until 3:00.
   a hopefully
   b definitely
   c personally

4 _____, I won't be sorry to see him go.
   a Personally
   b Definitely
   c Completely

5 He was always taking days off, so _____ , he lost his job.
   a really
   b definitely
   c not surprisingly

6 The meeting was very long, but _____ they got what they wanted.
   a completely
   b basically
   c personally

7 She's gone to live in Thailand for a year. _____ , she'll enjoy it.
   a Surprisingly
   b Personally
   c Hopefully

## Third Conditional

**3** Write Third Conditional sentences to describe how the situation could have been different. Use the prompts to start the new sentences.

I bought a new car. I didn't have enough money to go on holiday.

*If I hadn't bought a new car I would have had enough money to go on holiday.*

1 The manager was so difficult to work for. So we left the company.
   If the manager _____ .

2 I lost my phone. I didn't call you.
   I would have _____ .

3 It was a sunny day. We sat in the garden eating ice creams.
   We _____ .

4 She fell and broke her leg. She didn't become a professional dancer.
   If she _____ .

5 The train was delayed. He arrived late for work.
   He _____ .

6 I didn't read the contract carefully. I signed it.
   I wouldn't _____ .

7 I didn't remember my password. I couldn't use my email account.
   If I had _____ .

8 She lived by herself. She felt lonely.
   She _____ .

9 I signed up to Facebook. I met my wife on Facebook.
   I wouldn't _____ .

10 I had eaten too much. I felt sick.
   If I _____ .

## Vocabulary

**4** Complete the sentences with the expressions in the box and the verb *change*. Make sure you use the correct tense.

> her hairstyle    her name    ~~my career~~    my clothes
> my mind    the password    the subject

I have been thinking about my job and I think it's time to *change my career*.

1 I didn't recognise her at first because she's _____ . It's short now.

2 I wanted to go out but I've _____ . I'm going to stay at home.

3 I couldn't get into the computer programme, because you have _____ .

4 I asked you how much you spent. Don't _____ . I want to know!

5 She decided not to _____ when she got married, because her husband's surname is difficult to spell.

6 I'll be there in a minute. I just need to have a shower and _____ .

**5** Complete the text with words and phrases from the box.

> Basically    exhaust fumes    ~~global warming~~
> pollution    really    solar power

With temperatures rising all over the world, we know that *global warming* is a reality. Some people think this is a (1) _____ difficult problem to solve. Not me – I think it's simple. (2) _____ , all we have to do is treat it as our problem, not someone else's. Take energy, for example. We get most of it from big dirty power stations, which produce loads of (3) _____ . But that wouldn't happen if we used our common sense. If we all used (4) _____ by putting panels on our roofs to make our own electricity, it would make a huge difference. And if we used the bus instead of our car, our streets would not be so full of these disgusting (5) _____ .

**6** Correct one mistake in each sentence.

1 Extreme wealthy and poverty can be seen in many developing countries.

2 Luckily, they have found cure for this awful disease.

3 I think my standard living has improved since I came to this country.

4 I don't like the city because there is too much polluted.

5 Fortunately the mortal rate has fallen in recent years.

6 The use of solar power can help to reduce global warmings.

**7** Add a prefix and/or a suffix to the words in brackets to complete the sentences.

I can't trust him any more. He has been so *dishonest*. (honest)

1 This fish is _____ . It's almost raw. (cooked)

2 The _____ is responsible for education. (govern)

3 He went to a clinic for some private _____ . (treat)

4 Have you found some cheap _____ ? (accommodate)

5 He doesn't understand the _____ of saving money. (important)

6 A high level of _____ causes problems for the economy. (employ)

7 The United States of America declared its _____ on 4 July 1776. (independent)

8 There was a powerful student _____ in the 1970s. (move)

9 I don't think it will make any _____ . (different)

## How to...

**8** Add one word from the box to each line in the dialogue.

> a    about    from    if    right    to (x2)

1 A: What do you think about living in Bakewell? Is there anything you'd like change?

2 B: It would be nicer the weather was better.

3 A: Too! Definitely!

4 B: But there's not much we can do that.

5 A: Well, you have point there.

6 B: And there always seem be a lot of traffic jams.

7 A: That's certainly true. But apart that, I think it's fine. And I wouldn't want to live anywhere else.

## Vocabulary | jobs

**1** Use the clues to complete the crossword.

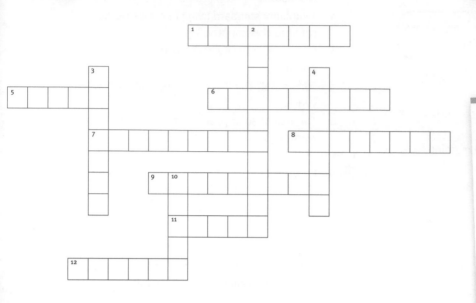

### Across

1 I need some extra money so I've offered to work o_____ this Saturday.
5 Most jobs involve some a_____ , like filling in forms and keeping records.
6 I used to work for a firm, but then I left to work f_____ , so now I'm my own boss.
7 A lot of mothers want a job with f_____ , so they can finish early some days to go and look after their children.
8 We're celebrating, because Magda has been p_____ . She's a manager now!
9 Most job v_____ are advertised online.
11 The pay is not very good, but we get some p_____ , like long holidays.
12 My annual s_____ is about 29,000 Euros.

### Down

2 They offered me the job after they checked my r_____ from my previous employer.
3 In some jobs, like the police, you have to wear a u_____ .
4 If I get the promotion, I should get a p_____ r_____ .
10 Are you going to a_____ for the job? I think you should – you'll probably get it.

## Grammar | make, let, allow

**2** Complete the email with the words from the box.

> allowed   allowed to   doesn't let
> let   make   makes

Hi Michele,

We're having great fun in London, except for the problems with our host family. The lady we are staying with is very strict and she (1) _____ us come home by 10:00 every evening, so we can't go out with the other students, which is a shame. We aren't (2) _____ to bring friends home either, and she (3) _____ us cook. We have to eat her cooking all the time, and it's terrible! The school is really good though, and we like our teachers. They (4) _____ us study hard, but we're (5) _____ choose which books we use, and they (6) _____ us talk in Spanish if we need to. Hope you're having a good time on the beach!

Lots of love

Marianna

## Pronunciation | intonation for pausing

**3** **a** Look at the dialogue. Divide each part into three sections, and show where you think the speaker will pause for emphasis.

A: I found this job advert last week and I decided it looks great – working outside and talking to people all day.

B: That's great – you're always saying you hate your job so why don't you apply?

A: I already have and guess what? I've got an interview tomorrow.

B: That's fantastic! I'm really pleased – I hope it goes well for you.

**b** 🔊 27 Listen and check.

# How to... | ask for clarification and deal with difficult questions

**4** **a** Complete the sentences with the words in the box.

> follow   like   said   say   saying   tell

a What I'd _____ to know is this. You _____ the company has spent too much this year, so what are you going to do about it?

b I didn't quite _____ what you just said about cuts. Are you _____ that staff won't get their pay rise this year?

c Yes, I've got one. Could you _____ me a bit more about our pay?

d I wonder if you could explain who will and who won't. Would it be true to _____ that managers like yourself are getting a pay rise, but ordinary employees like us aren't?

**b** Complete the dialogue by putting (a–d) from exercise 4a in the correct places (1–4).

**Gerald:** Anyway, do you have any questions?

**Sarah:** (1) _____

**Gerald:** Your pay? That's a very interesting question. What would you like to know?

**Sarah:** (2) _____

**Gerald:** What am I going to do? Well, let me think about that ... I suppose we'll have to spend less next year. Make cuts probably.

**Sarah:** (3) _____

**Gerald:** I'm not really sure if you'll get a pay rise or not. Some of us will get a pay rise, but we can't afford one for everyone.

**Sarah:** (4) _____

**Gerald:** That's a very interesting question. Er, I'm afraid I can't comment on my own pay. Ooh, look at the clock. It's time for lunch!

**c** 🔘 28 Listen and check.

# Reading

**5** **a** Read the blog. What is the most likely web address?

a Jobinterviewadvice.com

b Jobproblems.com

c Jobvacanciesonline.com

> **Posting 1** _____
> I've been doing the same job for ten years, but it's going nowhere. I'm bored and poorly paid, and the managers who are delegating jobs for me to do are much younger than me. I want to get a better job, but I won't be able to, because I haven't got a degree. It seems really unfair. *Annie*

> **Posting 2** _____
> My job involves controlling budgets and making decisions, and the work is challenging and enjoyable. We get on really well in the office and outside. The problem is that I'm in the office almost every day, because my manager is always asking us to come in at weekends. I don't want to say no, but the problem is that I hardly have any free time. Any advice? *Hassan*

> **Posting 3** _____
> I was promoted and became a manager last year. To be honest, it's not really 'me' to be delegating jobs to other people or interviewing job candidates. I'm not very good at making decisions or solving problems. I got on really well with my workmates before, but they're not so friendly towards me now. What should I do – just resign? *Javier*

**b** Match the titles (a–c) with the postings (1–3).

a My boss is always making me work overtime.

b I don't think I've got the right management skills

c I haven't got any formal qualifications – will this stop me getting a good job?

**6** Look at the replies to the postings. Complete the replies with the names of the writers (*Annie*, *Hassan* or *Javier*) in the postings in exercise 5.

> **Reply A**
> Not yet _____ , no. Ask if they can give you some management training – all firms should provide this if possible. Perhaps you're not ready for your new responsibilities yet. But give your new job a chance first. And don't worry about what your colleagues think! Good luck! *Keith*

> **Reply B**
> Hello _____ . I think you need to be more positive. If you don't apply, how will you know if they want you or not? If you don't have lots of exams you've done on your CV, write about all the skills you have instead. *Noreen*

> **Reply C**
> Hi _____ . Have you looked at your contract to see how many hours you should actually work? There must be something about your hours there. Also, if you say yes all the time, people probably think you're happy to do all the work. *Wildboy99*

## Vocabulary | -ing and -ed adjectives

**1** Complete the sentences with the words from the box.

> annoyed   bored   confusing   depressing
> excited   exhausted   frightened   frightening
> relaxing   tiring

1   I don't watch horror films. I find them too _____ .
2   I'm really _____ about starting my new job. It's going to be great.
3   It makes me sad. The news about the war is very _____ .
4   I was so _____ that I left the cinema before the film had finished.
5   When I am stressed, listening to music makes me feel better. It's very _____ .
6   I've been working long hours this week, so I'm _____ .
7   I don't understand these instructions. They are too _____ !
8   Frances was really _____ when she discovered we had spent all the money.
9   I have to carry lots of heavy boxes so my job is quite _____ .
10  She started screaming because she was _____ of spiders.

## Grammar | reported speech

**2** Complete the sentences with *say*, *tell* or *ask*. Make sure you use the correct tense.

1   Jesse _____ he would see us later.
2   The receptionist _____ us for our passports.
3   The bus driver _____ me where the station was.
4   I _____ her for her telephone number.
5   We _____ we wanted to stay for a week.
6   I _____ you that I would pay for the dinner.
7   He _____ me for the time.
8   I _____ him it was half past three.
9   I'll _____ my mother for some money.
10  I didn't know what to _____ to her.
11  He _____ me her name, but I didn't know.
12  He _____ that he had seen her before.
13  We got lost, so we had to _____ for directions.
14  Although he _____ me when the show starts, I've forgotten what he _____ .

**3** Read what Tran said last year and complete the reported sentences below. Make sure you use the correct tense.

My name is Tran and I come from Vietnam. I'm living in Sydney and working in a café. I've been here for three months and I really like it, but I miss my family and friends too. I want to go back home at Christmas, but I don't earn very much money so I can't afford the flight. I phoned my brother yesterday and he is going to visit me next month. Maybe I'll ask him to lend me some money! When I eventually go back to Vietnam, I will never forget my experiences here in Australia. I have made a lot of great friends, and my English has really improved.

1   He said that his name _____ Tran and he _____ Vietnam.
2   He said that he _____ in Sydney and _____ café.
3   He said that he _____ for three months and he _____ it, but he _____ his family and friends too.
4   He said that he _____ to go back home at Christmas, but he _____ very much money, so he _____ the flight.
5   He said that he _____ his brother _____ , and that he _____ to visit him the _____ month.
6   He said that maybe he _____ ask him _____ him some money.
7   He said that when he _____ to Vietnam, he _____ never forget his experiences in Australia.
8   He said that he _____ a lot of great friends.

## Reading

**4** Read the article and match the paragraphs (1–6) with the summary sentences (a–f).

a  Identify the danger signs
b  Understand why the manager is angry
c  Know where to stop

d  Don't meet anger with anger
e  What makes people angry at work?
f  Know where the anger is directed

# The boss from hell?

**1** _____

When you're at work, do you ever get angry? Yes? Then it's probably because of your manager. Bad management causes more people to lose their temper at work than any other reason. Almost four out of ten people across Europe said that poor management was the issue that makes them most angry about their jobs. In London, one out of three workers would describe their boss as 'the boss from hell'! Read our top tips to help you deal with an angry boss.

**2** _____

Some managers use fear as a management technique. They think it will make people respect them, although actually it just makes people want to leave their jobs.

**3** _____

Bosses like to get angry with new staff, to see if they can bully them. If you are new to a job, you need to work out if the anger is personal – because you have done something wrong, or business – this is how your manager treats all the new employees. You need to learn not to take things too personally.

**4** _____

Learn what are the particular things that make your boss angry. Does he go crazy when colleagues arrive late for work? Does he hate it when a job is not finished on time?

**5** _____

Sometimes the things you do will make other people angry. Learn to watch their reactions so that you can stop in time. If a colleague asks you to go outside for a fight, then you know you have gone too far!

**6** _____

Try breathing techniques to help you calm down. If someone is shouting at you, try imagining that you are blowing up a balloon. This allows your breathing to slow down and means you are less likely to get angry.

**5** Read the article again and find words or phrases in the article which mean …

1  get angry – lose your _____ (Paragraph 1)
2  bad management – _____ management (Paragraph 1)
3  cope with – _____ with (Paragraph 1)
4  a management strategy – a management _____ (Paragraph 2)
5  look up to someone – _____ them (Paragraph 2)
6  frighten someone who is smaller or weaker than you – _____ them (Paragraph 3)
7  decide after thinking carefully – _____ out (Paragraph 3)
8  get angry – go _____ (Paragraph 4)
9  become quiet instead of being angry – calm _____ (Paragraph 6)
10  the opposite of speed up – _____ down (Paragraph 6)

**6** Complete this summary of the article with the words and phrases from exercise 5.

The article describes how (1) _____ management is the main reason why people lose their (2) _____ at work, and it offers advice to help workers (3) _____ with a difficult boss. It explains how some managers use anger as a management (4) _____ in order to make employees (5) _____ them. Some bosses may (6) _____ new staff to see how they react. It is important to (7) _____ out why your boss is angry, so that you can try to avoid it. If this doesn't work, and your boss goes (8) _____ , the article suggests that you take deep breaths to help slow (9) _____ your breathing, and this will help you to (10) _____ down.

## Grammar | past obligation/permission

**1** **a** Choose the correct words in *italics*.

1 Were you allowed *leave/to leave* work early today?

2 *Could/Had* you wear whatever you wanted at school?

3 Did everyone in your country *have to/allowed* join the army?

4 Why *weren't/couldn't* you go back to work after you had your son?

5 *Were/Did* you allowed to stay out at night when you were a kid?

6 *Were/Could* you ask the computer engineer to help if you had problems at your last company?

7 Did you *have/could* to wait a long time to get a refund?

8 Were you allowed *to use/use* the Internet at school?

**b** Complete the sentences with the words from the box. Then match the questions (1–8) in exercise 1a with the answers (a–h).

> could   allowed (x2)   gave   had   have
> to   weren't

a Yes, but we _____ allowed to wear jeans or anything too casual.

b No, I always _____ to be back by 10:00 p.m.

c No, I didn't _____ to do military service.

d Because I had _____ look after him when he was little.

e Yes, the boss was in a good mood, so I was _____ to go home an hour early.

f Yes, but we were only _____ to use it for twenty minutes each time.

g No, they _____ me the money really quickly. They had to – I was so angry!

h Yes, we _____ ask them anything. They were really helpful.

## Vocabulary | job requirements

**2** Complete the job adverts with the words from the box.

> budgets   dealing   delegating   making
> persuading   qualifications   skills   stamina

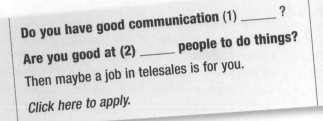

Do you have good communication (1) _____ ?

Are you good at (2) _____ people to do things?

Then maybe a job in telesales is for you.

*Click here to apply.*

**Childcare assistant needed**

No formal (3) _____ are necessary, but you will need a lot of (4) _____ , as children do require a lot of energy, as well as attention.

**Logtech International** are recruiting a Managing Director. Candidates who are used to (5) _____ hard decisions are invited to apply. Experience of management and (6) _____ work to your employees is essential.

**Senior Finance Director needed**

Must be good at (7) _____ with figures.
Needs to be able to control large (8) _____ .

# Listening

**3** **a** 🔵 29 Cover the audioscript. Listen to three people talking about their jobs. Look at the photos below and match the people (A–C) to the jobs (1–3).

A Tomoko

B Arnold

C Josefina

1 Music teacher
2 College careers advisor
3 Tour guide

**b** Listen again. What do the three people have in common? Tick (✓) the correct answer.

1 They all hate their jobs.
2 They all recently started a new job.
3 They have all been promoted.
4 They were all made redundant.

**c** Write the name of the person (Arnold, Josefina or Tomoko) who ...

1 is self-employed.
2 is a student.
3 says what their previous job was.
4 didn't like their previous job.

**d** Find words or phrases that describe ...

1 a job with exactly the same working hours every day (Arnold)
2 a job with changing working hours (Josefina)
3 benefit of a job (Tomoko)
4 deciding which jobs to do first (Tomoko)

## Lifelong learning | lexical cohesion

**4** Find the following in the audioscript:

1 two negative words Arnold uses to describe his old job.
2 two positive words Arnold uses to describe his new job.
3 four phrases Josefina uses to describe the children in her life.
4 three words Tomoko uses for talking about money.

---

**AUDIOSCRIPT**

**Arnold**

I was stuck in a nine-to-five job that I was really bored with. I was in the Human Resources department of a large company. I'd have to read hundreds of CVs every week, because of all the jobs we were advertising. I got quite interested in these CVs. And I started thinking about how I could help all these (mostly young) people write a better CV and get the best job possible. So that's what I do now for a living. I left the firm and last week I started helping our students get their first job. I advise them about job searching, help them with CVs and applications, that sort of thing. It's more satisfying, and I'm glad I made the change.

**Josefina**

I wanted to get back to work after my little boy was born. But even when I was working flexitime, it was difficult to have a family and a career. And I missed my boy when I was at work. So I've just set up a business of my own.

I run music classes for other parents with very young children. It's going really well, and best of all is that I get to spend more time with my son, even when I'm at work! And it's great to see all those little smiling faces!

**Tomoko**

My home town is full of visitors from overseas. I've just got my first paid job working for an agency, showing visitors round all the sights, meeting them from the airport and that sort of thing. It's enjoyable (perhaps the best perk is that I receive a wage for going to beautiful places!), and the people are really nice most of the time. You have to be good at prioritising tasks, like when there are two problems at the same time, and you need to decide which one to deal with first. There's the problem-solving too, like when there's a problem with hotel bookings or late flights. But it all makes the job more interesting. And the job provides a bit of an income while I do my course, which I'll finish next year.

---

# Vocabulary | UK and US English

**5** **a** Decide if the words are UK or US English. Write *UK* or *US*.

I mailed her a letter this morning. <u>*US*</u>

1 Let's go to the cinema and see a *film*. _____
2 I need to move out of my *apartment* on Friday. _____
3 He was driving at 150 k.p.h. along the *motorway*. _____
4 I'm tired. I really need a *vacation*. _____
5 Excuse me. Where is the *restroom*? _____
6 I'll see you in the *shopping centre*. _____
7 The car's running out of *gas*. We need to stop and fill up. _____
8 I need to recharge my *cell phone*. _____
9 I want to buy a cheap *return ticket* to New Zealand. _____

**b** Write the UK and US equivalents to the words in *italics* in exercise 5a.

mailed → posted

# Review and consolidation unit 9

## make, *let*, *allow*

**1** Correct the mistakes in the sentences, but keep the same verbs.

1. We not allowed to go into the conference hall.
2. She wouldn't let me to see a doctor.
3. They should to make her get a job.
4. Did they make you filling in a form?
5. Am I allow to smoking?
6. The landlord doesn't to let us have parties.
7. Her parents let to her to do anything she wants.
8. He's angry because we won't let he go to the cinema.

## Reported speech

**2** Complete the sentences with *say*/*tell*/*ask*. Make sure you use the correct tense. There may be more than one possibility.

1. My boyfriend _____ me to marry him!
2. We _____ her to meet us at the station.
3. The interviewer _____ us if we had enjoyed making the record.
4. Why didn't you _____ me before?
5. We _____ for some free tickets, but the manager _____ 'no'.
6. He _____ he would be here by two o'clock.
7. They _____ us whether we liked living in Edinburgh.
8. I _____ I would do the work as soon as possible.

**3** Choose the best option, a, b or c.

1. He _____ my daughter to be quiet.
   a said   b told   c asked to
2. She _____ it was the best holiday she had ever been on.
   a told   b said me   c said
3. They _____ that the boss would be late for the meeting.
   a told   b asked   c told me
4. 'I have been here for too long.'
   She told me that she _____ for too long.
   a had been there   b is there   c have been there
5. 'Would you like to come to my house for dinner?'
   She asked me whether I _____ to go to her house for dinner.
   a want   b will want   c wanted
6. 'I'll see you tomorrow.'
   He said he'd see me _____.
   a the next day   b that day   c this day
7. 'The car will be ready soon.'
   He said that the car _____ soon.
   a will be ready   b would be ready   c had been ready

## Past obligation/permission

**4** Complete the sentences with *could*/*couldn't*, *was(n't)*/*were(n't) allowed*, *had to*, *didn't have to*.

At school, we *had to* play outside in the rain. (It was necessary)

1. My brother _____ show his passport at customs. (It wasn't necessary)
2. As children, we _____ to talk at the dinner table. (It wasn't permitted)
3. We _____ play football every afternoon. (It was permitted)
4. I _____ to drive my father's car. (It wasn't permitted)
5. Unfortunately, we arrived late so we _____ sit at the back. (It was necessary)
6. The talk wasn't very interesting because we _____ ask questions. (It wasn't permitted)
7. I hope you _____ wait too long. (It wasn't necessary)
8. A few years ago, you _____ park for free anywhere in the city centre, but now you have to pay. (It was permitted)
9. We _____ work overtime yesterday, because several members of staff were ill. (It was necessary)
10. Recently, woman _____ be in the army in the UK. (It wasn't permitted)

## Vocabulary

**5** Choose the correct words in *italics*.

1. The advantage of my work is that I can work *rewarding*/*challenges*/*flexitime*.
2. One of the biggest *challenges*/*rewarding*/*pay rise* was learning a new language.
3. She works such *overtime*/*long hours*/*all day* that she should get a *promoted*/*rewarding*/*pay rise*.
4. He's been doing the job for years so he's very *rewarding*/*experienced*/*references*.
5. I'm *applying*/*experienced*/*promoted* for a new job, so I need to ask you for a *perks*/*CV*/*reference*.
6. JM just got *a job*/*pay rise*/*promoted* to senior manager.
7. The pay isn't very good. Are there any *perks*/*pay rise*/*references*?
8. I *retired*/*applied*/*worked* for a job as a police officer, but I didn't get it.

**6** Choose the correct words in *italics*.

1  If I am feeling *tired/tiring* at the end of the day, I have a bath and read my book.

2  Being a policeman can be quite *frightened/frightening* sometimes.

3  I can't wait to see you again after all this time. I'm so *exciting/excited*!

4  He never says 'please' or 'thank you'. It's really *annoying/annoyed*.

5  I'm not very good with figures. I find them too *confused/confusing*.

6  He's feeling a bit *depressed/depressing* because he can't find a job.

7  I have been working long hours, so I'm *exhausted/exhausting*.

8  My brother has probably got the most *bored/boring* job in the world.

9  I did some voluntary work last year, and I found it so *rewarded/rewarding*.

10  The documentary film was very *interesting/interested*.

**7** Complete the sentences with the words and phrases from the box.

> apply   delegating   overtime
> pay rise   perks   prioritise
> self-employed

1  I've decided to _____ for another job.

2  It's been a tiring week, because I've done twelve hours of _____ .

3  Most electricians are _____ , but a few work for building firms.

4  I have too many things to do, so I have to _____ which jobs are more urgent.

5  I try to do everything myself because I don't really like _____ jobs to my staff.

6  If we get a _____ , then I'll be able to afford to go out more often.

7  One of the _____ of my job is that we can work flexitime if we want.

# UK or US English

**8** **a** Complete the words in the sentences with the missing vowels.

1  I always take the *s_bw_y* to work in the morning. I find it's quicker.

2  Can I have the *b_ll*, please?

3  Would you like *ch_ps* or potatoes with your main course?

4  I sent off my *r_s_m_* for that job I told you about. Let's see if I hear anything.

5  Did you remember to *m_ _ l* that letter I told you about?

6  I'll see you in the *sh_pp_ng c_ntr_*.

7  I need to recharge my *c_ll ph_n_*.

8  Did you see that *f_lm* on TV last night?

9  I need to move out of my *_p_rtm_nt* on Friday.

10  Excuse me. Where is the *r_str_ _m*?

**b** Are the words you completed British English or American English?

**c** What is the UK or US English equivalent to the words in italics in sentences 1–10 in exercise 8a? Complete the table.

|     | UK          | US     |
|-----|-------------|--------|
| 1   | *underground* | *subway* |
| 2   |             |        |
| 3   |             |        |
| 4   |             |        |
| 5   |             |        |
| 6   |             |        |
| 7   |             |        |
| 8   |             |        |
| 9   |             |        |
| 10  |             |        |

# How to...

**9** Put the word in brackets in the correct place in the sentences.

I wonder you could explain that again, please. (if)
*I wonder if you could explain that again, please?*

1  Could you say that, please? (again)

_____

2  I didn't follow what you said about next week's meeting. (quite)

_____

3  Would it be true say you agree with the idea? (to)

_____

4  Well, let me think that before I give you an answer. (about)

_____

5  I'll have to get to you on that. (back)

_____

## Vocabulary | memories

**1** Choose the correct words in *italics*.

1 In my first week at university, I got *homesick/memorial* quite a lot.

2 We must *remind/remember* to buy some milk. We haven't got any left.

3 This house *reminds/remembers* me of the place where I used to live.

4 I keep this necklace as a *memento/nostalgia* of my grandmother.

5 Can you remind me *to/of* call Robin? I need to speak to him.

6 Why do people often feel *nostalgia/memory* for their childhood?

7 Do you *remind/remember* the day we met?

8 In my country, we put flowers on graves in *memory/remember* of the dead.

9 This programme reminds me *of/to* a film I saw last week.

10 In lots of European towns, you can see *memorials/commemorate* to people killed in the world wars.

## Lifelong learning | make it rhyme!

**2** **a** Find pairs of rhyming words from the box, and write them below.

> ~~call~~ debt get overtime password perk purred rhyme ~~shawl~~ trade unpaid work

*shawl* and *call*

_____ and _____

_____ and _____

_____ and _____

_____ and _____

_____ and _____

**b** Complete the sentences with the rhyming pairs in exercise 2a.

Give me a *call* if you want to borrow my *shawl*.

1 One _____ of my job is I can turn up to _____ whenever I want.

2 Look after your money, and don't _____ into _____ .

3 Lots of people in my _____ have to do quite a lot of _____ work, but at least it's fun!

4 I've changed my computer _____ to '_____', because I love cats, but don't tell anyone!

5 Does the word 'crime' _____ with the word '_____'?

## Grammar | *I wish/If only*

**3** Use two or three words to complete the second sentence of each pair so that it means the same as the first sentence.

1 We haven't got any matches to light the fire.
I wish _____ some matches.

2 I can't afford that skirt.
I wish _____ that skirt.

3 She is very sad that she missed your wedding.
She wishes _____ your wedding.

4 You always make a mess in the kitchen!
I wish _____ make a mess in the kitchen!

5 We were late for the train, so then we missed our flight!
If only _____ late for the train!

6 You live too far away, so we never see each other.
If only _____ closer to me.

7 I can't do this Biology homework. It's too difficult.
I _____ better at Biology.

8 I love China but I can't speak the language.
I wish _____ Chinese.

9 I ate a disgusting pizza.
I wish _____ that pizza.

10 You're always complaining!
I wish _____ stop complaining!

**4** What do these people wish? Write sentences using the phrases from the box.

> not be so short    not buy this car
> have more money    revise    can run faster
> not go skiing

# Reading

**5** **a** What do you think a 'brain pill' does?

1 Destroys bad memories

2 Improves your memory

Now read the article to check.

# Instant Memory

**1** _____

Imagine the scene: you have an important exam tomorrow morning. Your future depends on it. You stay up all night, drinking endless cups of coffee, trying to memorise four years' information in twelve hours. Sounds familiar? But imagine you didn't need to do this. Imagine you could just take a brain pill and immediately remember everything.

**2** _____

A memory pill, or any other pill that wakes up the brain, is a great idea, not only for students, but for lots of other professions. Soldiers, who have to function with just a few hours' sleep, would welcome it. So would pilots on long trips, and shift workers who have to work with heavy machines at night. So too would the 37 million people around the world who suffer from Alzheimer's Disease, an illness that robs people of their memory.

**3** _____

But are we close to finding such a pill? A number of pharmaceutical companies are already working on it. They see enormous financial possibilities in a pill that increases the memory, and laboratories have already been testing pills on both animals and humans.

**4** _____

But a memory pill raises ethical questions too. Research tells us that the pill would be used not only by ill people, but also by people who just wanted to remember everyone's name at parties, or the laziest students. Is this fair on poorer students who couldn't afford the pill? Would businesses start asking their workers to take pills so that they performed better? Would we divide quiz shows into two types: contestants with brain pills and contestants without?

**5** _____

Medicine and its processes evolve. Often, the original purpose gets lost. This has happened with plastic surgery (originally for soldiers with injuries to the face; now used by middle-aged actors who want to stay prettier for longer) and it happened with Prozac. It may happen with cloning. The truth is, we don't know how a memory pill would affect society. Fortunately, we probably have a few more years to think about it. Most scientists believe that the drugs need much more testing. Some of these drugs work well with animals, but, as Dr Sue Clarke, one of the scientists working in this area, says, 'It isn't clear that animals use the same kind of memories as humans. A mouse doesn't have to remember a shopping list during the day.'

**b** Match the headings (a–e) with the paragraphs (1–5).

a What usually happens with medicine?

b Questions society needs to ask

c The solution for exam students!

d Who needs a 'brain pill' at work?

e Big businesses searching for 'brain pill'

**c** Match the users (1–4) with the benefits they could get from brain pills (a–d).

Users

1 soldiers

2 students

3 pharmaceutical companies

4 party guests

Benefits

a remember facts more quickly

b learn more people's names

c manage with less sleep

d make more money

**6** Complete the summary of the text. Use one word in each gap.

Brain pills would be welcomed by students who were studying for (1) _____ . Many professions would also use them: for example, people who (2) _____ in shifts and pilots and soldiers who don't get much (3) _____ . But brain pills raise many (4) _____ too, about how society would use them. Many scientists say that the pill needs to be (5) _____ more, before we can use it safely.

## Vocabulary | biographies

**1** Read the article about a famous athlete, and put the words in brackets in the correct order.

Prasanta Karmakar is (widely be to considered) _widely considered to be_ one of India's most talented athletes. But he had (life a start in difficult) (1) _____ , as he lost an arm as a child. (From early age an) (2) _____ he wanted to be a great swimmer, and worked hard (odds against the) (3) _____ to achieve this. He is perhaps (known for best) (4) _____ being the first Indian swimmer to win a medal at the Commonwealth Games.

## Grammar | review of past tenses

**2** Choose the correct verb tense in *italics*.

1 When he retired from international football, David Beckham *was playing/had played* for England 115 times.

2 When Lady Gaga appeared on the front page of *Time* magazine in May 2010, she *had already sold/was already selling* fifteen million albums worldwide.

3 Hardworking Taiwanese pop star, Jay Chou, would often sleep at the studio while he *was recording/had recorded* songs.

4 Julia Roberts made her first film at twenty. Before that she *was being/had been* a model.

5 President Kennedy was shot while his car *was driving/had driven* through Dallas on 22 November, 1963.

**3** Complete the sentences with the Past Continuous or Past Perfect form of the verbs in brackets.

1 After we _____ (know) Michelle for a few months, we invited her over for lunch.

2 Paul arrived four hours late. He explained that his car _____ (break down) in Lyon.

3 Oh sorry, _____ (you/talk) to me?

4 When they arrived, it was hot because Mrs Blofeld _____ (switch on) the heating.

5 We _____ (wait) for the bus when it started raining.

6 I first began getting these headaches while I _____ (listen) to rock music.

7 Scotland was completely new to Max. He _____ (not/go) there before.

**4** Complete the text with the Past Simple, Past Continuous or Past Perfect form of the verbs in brackets.

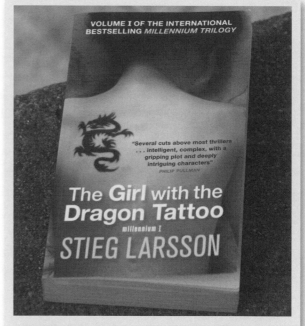

When Swedish author Stieg Larsson died in 2004, very few people (1) _____ (hear) of him. But within just a few years, almost everyone (2) _____ (know) who he was. In 2009, the author of the three Millenium books (3) _____ (become) the best-selling author in Europe. By October 2010, his books (4) _____ (sell) 30 million copies worldwide. So who was this man? Larsson (5) _____ (work) as a magazine editor during the day. Writing novels was just a hobby, which he (6) _____ (do) in the evenings. He wrote on his computer while his partner (7) _____ (prepare) their evening meal. In fact, many of his work colleagues did not know he (8) _____ (write) a book at all.

# Pronunciation | pronouncing numbers

**5** Correct the words which do not match the numbers.

|  | 2.5% | two point five percent ✓ |
|---|---|---|
| 1 | 1,000,000 | one billion |
| 2 | 1970s | the ninety seventies |
| 3 | 03/04/11 | the third of April, two thousand and eleven |
| 4 | 1,298 | twelve thousand and ninety-eight |
| 5 | 3/4 | three fours |
| 6 | $18.20 | eighteen dollars and twenty cents |
| 7 | 99.9% | ninety-nine and nine percent |
| 8 | C20th | the twentieth century |
| 9 | 40,000 | forty thousand |
| 10 | 1969 | nineteen ninety-six |
| 11 | 11½ | eleven and half |

**6 a** Write these words in numbers.

Four hundred and six *406*

1 Sixteen thousand, three hundred and forty-nine
2 A third
3 Fourteen percent
4 The third of December two thousand and eleven
5 Eighty-eight dollars, seventy-one cents
6 The nineteen nineties

**b** Write these numbers and dates in words.

£45.20 – *forty-five pounds, twenty pence*

1 £23,993

2 3/4

3 99.8%

4 1990s

5 30/12/07

6 20th century

7 16/01/2011

8 €2.20

# How to... | say numbers

**7 a** 🔘 30 Cover the audioscript. Listen to the sentences. <u>Underline</u> the number or date that you hear.

| | a | | b | |
|---|---|---|---|---|
| 1 | a | 4,998 | b | 4,989 |
| 2 | a | £75.99 | b | £79.99 |
| 3 | a | 60% | b | 50% |
| 4 | a | 16/12/12 | b | 15/11/12 |
| 5 | a | 6 ½ | b | 16 ½ |
| 6 | a | 1990s | b | 1980s |
| 7 | a | 21st century | b | 20th century |
| 8 | a | 10th January 1969 | b | 10th July 1969 |
| 9 | a | 1,000 | b | 1,000,000 |
| 10 | a | $1,845 | b | $1,345 |

**AUDIOSCRIPT**

1 There were four thousand, nine hundred and ninety-eight people at the conference.
2 It costs seventy-nine pounds, ninety-nine pence, which is quite cheap really.
3 We are expecting a fifty percent increase in sales.
4 The programme starts on the fifteenth of November, two thousand and twelve.
5 I've had the car for about six and a half years now.
6 I listen to a lot of music from the nineteen-eighties.
7 There have been changes in transport, even since the beginning of the twenty-first century.
8 I was born on the tenth of July, nineteen sixty-nine.
9 A million men came to Washington that day.
10 This washing machine costs one thousand three hundred and forty-five dollars.

**b** 🔘 31 Now read aloud the numbers and dates you underlined in exercise 7a. Listen and check.

**AUDIOSCRIPT**

1 Four thousand, nine hundred and ninety-eight
2 Seventy-nine pounds, ninety-nine pence
3 Fifty percent
4 The fifteenth of November, two thousand and twelve
5 Six and a half years
6 The nineteen-eighties
7 The twenty-first century
8 The tenth of July, nineteen sixty-nine
9 A million
10 One thousand, three hundred and forty-five

## Grammar | phrasal verbs

**1** Choose the correct words in *italics*.

1 I hope they turn *in/up* on time. They were late last week.
2 I'm going *through/in* a difficult time at work.
3 Excuse the interruption. Please carry *over/on* what you were doing.
4 He called *round/off* the wedding. She was really upset.
5 I hope you can come *up/at* with some better ideas than that!
6 She split *up/off* with her husband two months after the wedding.
7 I can't put *up/on* with your behaviour any more! It's got to stop!
8 Strange things go *in/on* in this town all the time.
9 If I leave now, I'll never come *off/back*.
10 We need to find *up/out* what time the train leaves.

## Pronunciation | word stress in phrasal verbs

**2** 🔵 32 Listen to the sentences in exercise 1 and <u>underline</u> the part of the phrasal verb which is stressed.

## Grammar | phrasal verbs

**3** Read the email. There are six mistakes (including the example). Find and correct the mistakes.

| From: | Tom |
|---|---|
| To: | Jason |

Hi Jason,

It was great to hear from you again. I've got some good news and some bad news. You remember I told you about my wedding to Maria next month? Well, I'm afraid I've ~~called off it~~ *called it off*. Maria and I were going a difficult time through. Actually, I don't think she could put up my awful jokes with! But seriously, I think she's already got it over, and she's already found a new boyfriend! So that's good.

You'll never guess who turned at my office up the other day. Janet from school! Do you remember her? The one all the boys were in love with! Anyway, I found out she was abroad for a few years, but came last month back. So now we work together. And best of all: I'm taking her out to dinner tomorrow night!

Take care and hope to see you soon.

Regards,

Tom

## How to... | say goodbye (in person)

**4** Choose the correct word in *italics*.

1 Right, well it's time I *making/made* a move.
2 I'm *off/down*.
3 Thank you very much for *come/coming*.
4 *Have/Having* a safe trip.
5 Thanks for a great evening – I *enjoyed really/really enjoyed* it.
6 We'll see you in a *few/couple* of weeks.
7 Maybe *see/look at* you next weekend.

## Vocabulary | the senses

**5** Match the sentence beginnings (1–5) with the sentence endings (a–e).

1 Can you hear the birds
2 That sounds like a
3 Your dress looks
4 I just love the smell
5 This tastes

a of food cooking slowly.
b beautiful on you.
c really great idea.
d absolutely delicious.
e singing in the trees?

**5** Use a phrasal verb to replace the words in *italics*. Make sure you use the correct tense.

I don't know what *is happening* <u>is going on</u> at work. The boss has left, but we haven't (1) *discovered* who is going to replace him. We can't (2) *continue* like this, though. We are (3) *having* the worst economic crisis in years, and there's no one in charge! Actually, I hope the old boss (4) *returns*. He's better than nobody.

Mary suddenly (5) *appeared* at my door in tears yesterday. She was so sad. She told me that she had (6) *ended her relationship* with Bob. I'm not sure why, but maybe she couldn't (7) *tolerate* his bad manners any longer. I can't (8) *think of* any other reasons. They've had to (9) *cancel* the wedding.

## Vocabulary

**6** <u>Underline</u> the sentence endings which are not possible.

1 I love the sound
  a of the rain.   b like a drum.
  c of children playing.

2 Can you remind me
  a to call Judy?   b of my friend?
  c to send that email?

3 This food tastes
  a like cheese.   b delicious.
  c a type of fruit.

4 I've lost
  a the taste of apples.   b my watch.
  c some money.

5 That reminds me of
  a my grandmother.   b go home.
  c last weekend.

6 She doesn't like
  a the feel of wool.   b feeling of stone.
  c feeling tired.

7 It sounds
  a like a great book.   b fantastic.
  c of England.

8 Don't forget
  a buying milk.   b your towel.
  c to send me a postcard.

9 I can't remember
  a anything.   b my neighbour.
  c of that film.

10 You look
  a a model.   b very beautiful.
  c like my sister.

## Listening

**6** **a** Which of these are good ways of remembering vocabulary? Which ones do you use?

a Review new words regularly (almost every day). ☐
b Stick notes around your house with new words on them. ☐
c Test yourself regularly. ☐
d Use new words in class whenever you can. ☐
e Draw pictures of words and phrases. ☐
f Read your notes before you go to bed. ☐

**b** 🔘 33 Cover the audioscript. Listen to two language students discussing how to remember things they learn. Number the things in exercise 6a in the order that they are mentioned.

**c** Listen again and choose the best answer, a or b.

1 What is their relationship?
  a They are classmates.
  b He is her teacher.

2 What language are they learning?
  a Japanese.
  b Italian.

3 Where does the woman write new words?
  a On little notes and in a notebook.
  b On the bedroom walls.

4 Why should you write new words in your own sentences?
  a Because then you will dream of the words.
  b Because you can remember them better.

5 What does the woman think is the most important thing for learning new words?
  a Draw pictures of the words.
  b Revise regularly.

6 Who uses the most learning strategies?
  a The man.
  b The woman.

**7** How were the following things connected to suggestions for language learning?

**a fridge** – *the woman sticks words onto her fridge to help her remember them*

1 a train journey

_____

2 bedtime

_____

3 family and friends

_____

4 drawing pictures

_____

5 language lessons

_____

# Answer key

## I wish/If only

**1** Look at the dialogues. Complete B's response to A.

1 A I want to be there with you, but I'm too busy.
   B I wish you _____ here too.
   a were   b are   c will be

2 A You're very lazy and your room's a mess and you haven't done your homework.
   B I wish you _____ criticising me.
   a stop   b will stop   c would stop

3 A Our exam is on Thursday.
   B If only we _____ to do this exam!
   a didn't have   b don't have
   c wouldn't have

4 A You didn't have to buy those new chairs. I've already ordered a new sofa.
   B That's great! I wish you _____ me earlier.
   a had told   b told   c would tell

5 A I'm sorry, but there's no room for all your friends to stay.
   B Oh, Mum! If only we _____ a bigger house.
   a had had   b had   c would have

6 A You have to keep working. All of this must be finished by five o'clock.
   B If only I _____ a break now!
   a can have   b could have   c would have

7 A You're too young to come in here.
   B If only I _____ older!
   a wasn't   b am   c was

8 A That film was absolutely terrible, wasn't it?
   B Yes. I wish we _____ our money on such rubbish!
   a don't waste   b hadn't wasted
   c won't waste

**2** Complete the second sentence of each pair using the verbs in brackets so that it means the same as the first sentence.

I love tennis, but I'm not very good. (be)
I wish _was_ better at tennis.

1 I hate smoking but I can't give up! (be able to stop)
   I wish I _____ smoking.

2 That lottery ticket was the winner, but you threw it away! (throw away)
   If only you _____ the ticket!

3 Unfortunately I didn't buy any insurance before I was robbed. (buy)
   I wish I _____ insurance before I was robbed.

4 Stupidly, I forgot to take my keys with me. (take)
   If only I _____ my keys.

5 I'm afraid I can't remember her name. (be able to remember)
   I wish I _____ her name.

## Unit 1 Friends

### Lesson 1.1

**Vocabulary** | friends

**1**
1 keep in touch  2 a good sense of humour  3 ex-girlfriend  4 friend of a friend  5 get to know her  6 colleagues  7 have a lot in common  8 on the same wavelength  9 best friend  10 lost touch

**2**
1 in  2 about  3 about  4 on  5 at  6 in  7 on

**Grammar** | auxiliary verbs (*do, be, have*)

**3a**
1 Are you good at sports?  2 Has he got any brothers or sisters?  3 How old are they?  4 Do you like studying German?  5 Have you been to America?  6 Have you seen your boss today?  7 Did you go to the shops yesterday?

**3b**
1 Yes, I am./No, I'm not.  2 Yes, he has./No, he hasn't.  3 Possible answer: My sister's 20 years old and my brother's 22.  4 Yes, I do./No, I don't.  5 Yes, I have./No, I haven't.  6 Yes, I have./No, I haven't.  7 Yes, I did./No, I didn't.

**4a**
1 What sports are you interested in?  2 Have you been skiing recently?  3 Does she like listening to music?  4 Did Mozart play the violin?  5 Did your parents enjoy the concert last night?  6 Has Clara had her baby yet?  7 Were you born in Turin?  8 Did you speak to Frances yesterday?

**4b**
a 3  b 7  c 8  d 5  e 4  f 1  g 6  h 2

**Pronunciation** | intonation in echo questions

**5a**
1 h  2 b  3 e  4 f  5 a  6 d  7 g  8 c

**5c**
1 friendly and interested  2 bored  3 friendly and interested  4 annoyed  5 friendly and interested  6 annoyed  7 friendly and interested  8 bored

**Reading**

**6**
3 is the best title

**7**
1 F  2 T  3 F  4 T

**8**
1 c  2 b

### Lesson 1.2

**Vocabulary** | personality

**1**
1 kind-hearted  2 jealous  3 encouraging  4 upbeat  5 sulky  6 mean  7 dependable  8 pleasant

**2**
1 a  2 b  3 a  4 a  5 a

**Pronunciation** | sounds and spelling: *ea*

**3a**
1 heart  2 meat  3 each  4 colleague  5 season

**3c**

| /iː/ | /e/ | /ɪə/ | /aː/ |
|---|---|---|---|
| cheap<br>meat (x2)<br>mean<br>teacher<br>upbeat<br>disease<br>each<br>colleague<br>season | jealous<br>healthier<br>breakfast<br>read<br>weather<br>pleasant | really<br>fearful<br>year<br>clear<br>realised<br>ear<br>theatre | heart |

**How to...** | start a conversation with a stranger

**4**
1 haven't  2 are  3 Have  4 couldn't  5 Do  6 do

**5**
a 6  b 2  c 1  d 3  e 5  f 4

**Grammar** | Present Simple and Present Continuous

**6**
1 I'm not understanding (I don't understand)  2 Are you wanting (Do you want)  3 Correct  4 He's having (He has)  5 Correct  6 Correct  7 Correct  8 I'm knowing (I know)

**7**
1 's getting  2 finish ... takes  3 's getting  4 Do ... listen  5 'm living  6 's raining

**Listening**

**8a**
2

**8b**
1 b  2 b  3 a  4 a  5 a  6 b  7 b  8 a

### Lesson 1.3

**Vocabulary** | arguing

**1a**
1 c  2 a  3 g  4 b  5 f  6 d  7 e

**1b**
José and the writer

**1c**
José was my best friend at school. But one day we had **an** argument about money. I remember I got really angry **with** him. I said some horrible things to him. He lost **his** temper and shouted at me. We completely **fell** out, and didn't speak to each other **for** years after that. That was all many years ago now.
And now? Well, believe it or not, my son has just married José's daughter! And José and I are **in** touch every day, just like before.

**Grammar** | Present Perfect Simple and Past Simple

**2**
1 have always admired  2 looked after  3 finished  4 has lived  5 spent  6 met  7 have been married  8 moved  9 have never been  10 have just bought

**3**
1 have kept dogs since  2 has been in Paris for  3 have known them for  4 has had that car for  5 has lived in the countryside since

**Grammar** | *for, since, ago, already, just & yet*

**4**
1 ✓  2 ✓  3 since (for)  4 for (since)  5 since (for)  6 ✓  7 since (for)

**5**
1 already  2 just  3 for  4 yet  5 since  6 ago

**Vocabulary** | phrasal verbs

**6**
1 brought  2 after  3 looked  4 on  5 after  6 got  7 told  8 up

**Reading**

**7**
2

**8**
1 F  2 T  3 T  4 NG  5 F  6 NG  7 NG

### Review and consolidation unit 1

#### Auxiliary verbs (*do, be, have*)

**1**
1 Do you live in Thailand?  2 Did you see the James Bond film last night?  3 When is Sal going on holiday?/When does Sal go on holiday?  4 What sports are you interested in?  5 Do you enjoy studying?  6 Have you forgotten your books?  7 Does Tim like working for IBM?  8 Are you happy in your new flat?  9 Did George have a good time at the party yesterday?  10 Have you passed all your exams?

## Present tenses

**2**

1 fly  2 do  3 are  4 doesn't seem  5 've just finished  6 's talking  7 'm trying  8 've always enjoyed  9 can't remember

**3**

1 Have … been  2 went  3 Did … enjoy  4 thought  5 Do … play  6 'm/am  7 have … played/been playing  8 started  9 Do … want  10 sounds

**4**

1 for  2 since  3 since  4 for  5 since  6 for  7 since  8 for  9 since  10 since

**5**

1 know (known)  2 spoke (spoken)  3 have they got (did they get)  4 since (for)  5 started (start)  6 did see (seen)  7 never (ever)  8 have (has)  9 start (started)  10 did sign (signed)

### Vocabulary

**6**

1 f  2 e  3 d  4 c  5 h  6 a  7 b  8 g

**7**

1 got  2 had  3 had  4 got  5 had  6 had  7 get

**8**

1 selfish  2 jealous  3 dependable  4 pleasant  5 mean  6 encouraging

**9**

1 told  2 over  3 up to  4 after  5 up  6 up  7 grew  8 on  9 in  10 after

### How to…

**10**

1 Is it always this crowded?  2 So, how do you know Sara?  3 Have you tried these sandwiches?  4 Excuse me, could you tell me the time?

# Unit 2 Media

## Lesson 2.1

### Vocabulary | media

**1a**

1 reality  2 instant  3 horror  4 thriller  5 romantic  6 current
a soaps  b online  c gossip  d gripping  e moving  f period

**1b**

1 a  2 b  3 f  4 d  5 e  6 c

### Vocabulary | film

**2**

1 thriller  2 romantic comedy  3 docu-drama  4 animated film  5 period drama  6 horror film

### Grammar | defining relative clauses

**3**

1 b That's the man whose wife won the lottery.  2 f I like people who are always honest.  3 c I've got an old care which never goes wrong.  4 a Ella works in a factory which makes jewellery.  5 d Laguna has a beach where you can surf all year.  6 e I spoke to the architect who's designing my house.

**4a**

1 where  2 which  3 who  4 which  5 where  6 whose

**4b**

1 F – New York  2 T  3 F – Morgan Spurlock  4 T  5 F – Élysée Palace  6 T

### How to… | give opinions and disagree

**5**

1 reckon  2 opinion  3 sure  4 true  5 on  6 What  7 sense  8 do

### Lifelong learning | using the media!

**6**

1 Do you ever instant message your friends?  2 How often do you go to the cinema?  3 What's the best film you've ever seen?  4 Do you know anyone who's been on TV?  5 What's the funniest comedy you've ever seen?  6 What's the best way to learn about current affairs?

### Reading

**7a**

2

**7b**

1 F  2 T  3 F  4 T  5 F  6 T

## Lesson 2.2

### Vocabulary | television

**1**

1 d  2 a  3 e  4 c  5 f  6 b

### Pronunciation | /n/ and /ŋ/

**2a**

/ŋ/: chatting evening entertaining bank banks singing boring exciting

### Grammar | the passive

**3**

1 are written by  2 was made by  3 was organised by  4 has been signed  5 will be covered  6 be found  7 are bought by Australians (in Australia)  8 were sold

### How to… | describe an object

**4**

1 for  2 of  3 to  4 by  5 like  6 of

**5**

1 a TV remote control  2 a coin  3 the word *nauseating*  4 headphones  5 a calculator  6 a notebook

### Reading

**6a**

1 b  2 a  3 b  4 c  5 c  6 b  7 c

**6b**

1 hackers  2 star reporter  3 fired  4 insisted  5 under pressure  6 celebrities

## Lesson 2.3

### Pronunciation | word stress on word endings

**1a**

1 different  2 different  3 same  4 different  5 different

### Grammar | Past Simple and Past Continuous

**2**

1 were looking  2 found  3 went  4 was  5 were worrying  6 spent  7 was brushing  8 said  9 stopped  10 was driving

**3**

1 stole … wasn't looking  2 didn't know … were  3 didn't hear … were listening  4 was driving . … saw  5 didn't take … was  6 met … were skiing

### Vocabulary | in the news

**4a**

1 c  2 b  3 a  4 e  5 d

**4b**

a 4  b 3  c 5  d 2  e 1

### Listening

**5a**

1 fat  2 homes  3 Taxi driver  4 rock star (Lee Santana)

**5b**

1 900 children aged 11 to 15  2 Hamburgers, chips, chocolate and fizzy soft drinks.  3 A shopping area and a car park.  4 Next year.  5 A husband and wife.  6 To a London hospital.  7 In an art gallery (in Manchester).  8 Extremely happy.

## Review and consolidation unit 2

### Defining relative clauses

**1**

1 Los Angeles is the city where Michael Jackson died.  2 Franz Kafka was the writer who wrote a story about a man who became an insect.  3 St Petersburg is the city which used to be called Leningrad.  4 Rodin was the sculptor who made *The Thinker*.  5 *Avatar* is a famous film which cost $500,000,000 to make.  6 Malibu is the beach in California where hundreds of celebrities live.  7 Vivaldi was the composer whose most famous work was *The Four Seasons*.  8 Istanbul is the city which is built on two continents – Europe and Asia.

**2**

1 who was given  2 which (or that) are told  3 whose paintings are sold  4 where I was born  5 which/that can be used  6 whose bags have been

**5**

1 Who did give (gave) Mina my email address? 2 Correct 3 Who (does) the book belong to? 4 Who did invent (invented) the computer? 5 Correct 6 Correct 7 Where does lives Marianna (live)? 8 What did happen (happened) at the meeting?

### Reading

**6**

1 a 2 c 3 d 4 b

**7**

1 mistakes 2 children 3 the fear of success 4 starting to worry and deciding not to take risks

**8**

1 bother 2 falling over 3 mispronouncing 4 juggle 5 keys 6 draw outside the lines 7 take risks 8 opportunities

## Lesson 7.2

**Vocabulary** | personal qualities

**1**

1 encouraging 2 inspiring 3 patient 4 boring 5 understanding

**Vocabulary** | word building

**2**

1 boredom 2 clarify 3 tolerant 4 frighten 5 knowledgeable 6 patience

**Pronunciation** | word stress in word building

**3b**

Column A: encourage, decision, electric, artistic, musician
Column B: interesting, frightening, scientist, educate

**Grammar** | used to and would

**4**

1 I used to/would spend my holidays with my grandparents. 2 My grandmother would/used to cook delicious meals. 3 She used to keep chickens, goats and horses. 4 My cousin and I used to/would ride the horses every day. 5 My favourite horse was called Racer. 6 Racer used to be faster than all the other horses. 7 I didn't use to understand how dangerous riding could be. 8 One day I fell off Racer and broke my arm. 9 My mother didn't/wouldn't let me ride him again. 10 After that, I used to/would sit in the house and watch sadly as the horses played in the field.

**5a**

1 I used to play volleyball when I was at school. 2 Did Sylvie use to smoke? 3 I didn't use to like mushrooms. I love them now. 4 I used to enjoy cooking. Now I don't have enough time. 5 She used to drink milk when she was a child but know she's allergic to it. 6 He didn't use to play computer games before. Now he is always playing them. 7 I used to read a lot of books when I was at university. I don't read so many now. 8 You don't study there now, but did you use to go to the Anglo-American school?

### Listening

**6**

1 He didn't know much about school, and wasn't interested in going. 2 The art of keeping still. 3 He was probably frightened of them.

**7**

1 T 2 F 3 F 4 F 5 T 6 F 7 F 8 F 9 T 10 T

## Lesson 7.3

**Vocabulary** | education

**1**

1 subject 2 blended 3 academic 4 take 5 course 6 learning 7 continuous 8 seminar

**Grammar** | modals of ability, past and present

**2**

1 could paint 2 was able to tell 3 managed to write 4 was able to read 5 managed to publish 6 can play

**Pronunciation** | connected speech

**3**

1 a 2 b 3 a 4 b

**How to...** | carry out an interview

**4a**

1 Would you mind telling me how much you earn per day? 2 I wonder if you could tell me why you decided to become a dancer? 3 Can you give me an example of a dance that was difficult to learn? 4 And how did you learn to do that?

**4b**

1 c 2 a 3 d 4 b

**Vocabulary** | learning: idioms and phrasal verbs

**5**

1 cake 2 gave 3 wild 4 up 5 teacher's 6 bookworm 7 brush 8 out 9 learn 10 colours

### Reading

**6**

Title 3 is best.

**7**

56 years: the number of years Dorothy Beckett has worked in the cake factory. 4 million: the annual turnover for the cake business. 20: the number of years of experience that Javier has a web designer. 71: Javier's age when he retired. 70: many of the other workers are 70 years younger than Dorothy Beckett. 40 hours: the number of hours Dorothy Beckett works a week. 91: Javier's age now

**8**

1 Three things that people can do when they stop working are gardening, taking holidays and chatting with friends. 2 Her work involves putting cakes in boxes. 3 Some are 23 years old. 4 No, she says she never wants to retire. 5 After he retired. 6 His clients won't let him retire. 7 Yes, he really likes it.

## Review and consolidation unit 7

### Subject and object questions

**1**

1 Who did go (went) to the meeting? 2 Correct 3 What did happen (happened)? 4 Where did (was) Shakespeare born? 5 Who did write (wrote) *The Castle*? 6 Correct 7 Who did telephone (telephoned) the engineer? 8 Correct 9 Correct 10 Who did eat (ate) the cake?

### *used to* and *would*/ Past Simple

**2**

1 b 2 b 3 b and c 4 a and b 5 a 6 c 7 a and c 8 b

### Modals of ability, past and present

**3**

1 managed 2 couldn't 3 able 4 manage 5 couldn't 6 manage to 7 couldn't 8 wasn't able 9 could 10 couldn't

### Lifelong learning (using a correction code)

**4**

I decided to brush out [WW – up] on my German before my holiday to germany [1 P – Germany], and enrolled on an intensive course at my college local [2 WO – local college]. It was a pretty steap [3 Sp – steep] learning curve, and I was amazed how much I'd forgotten from [4 WW – since] my at school time [5 WO – my time at school]. In those days, I've been [6 WT – was] quite good, and I knew the grammar inside out. At [7 M – the] end of the corse [8 Sp – course] there had been [9 WT – was] a test. It was all multiple choice. When I didn't know [10 M – an] answer, I just made a wild guessing [11 WF – guess]. Well, I must be the world's best guesser, because somehow I passed with fly [12 WF – flying] colours. I've no idea how I did it? [13 P – .]

## Vocabulary

**5**

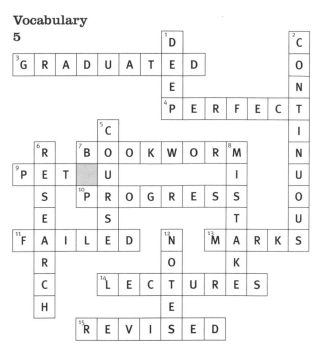

Crossword:
- 3 across: GRADUATED
- 4 across: PERFECT
- 7 across: BOOKWORM
- 9 across: PET
- 10 across: PROGRESS
- 11 across: FAILED
- 13 across: MARKS
- 14 across: LECTURES
- 15 across: REVISED
- 1 down: D E E P
- 2 down: C O N T I N U O U S
- 5 down: C U S
- 6 down: R E S E S E
- Down: F A R C H

**6**

1 fast learner  2 strict  3 Practice … perfect  4 steep … curve  5 heart
6 picked  7 thrown … deep  8 brought

**7**

1 knowledgeable  2 understanding  3 strict  4 patient  5 clarify
6 encouragement

### How to…

**8**

1 wonder  2 though  3 know  4 sounds  5 surprised  6 interest

# Unit 8 Change

## Lesson 8.1

### Vocabulary | change

**1**

1 password  2 climate  3 career  4 mind  5 subject  6 hairstyle

### Grammar | Second Conditional

**2**

1 'll  2 wouldn't  3 stops  4 had  5 would be  6 asked  7 would  8 won't

**3**

1 d  2 f  3 e  4 a  5 h  6 g  7 b  8 c

### Vocabulary | cities

**4**

1 building  2 congestion  3 rush hour  4 honking  5 exhaust  6 traffic
jams

### How to… | discuss problems and suggest changes

**5a**

Four things the person would like: have more time; have three-day
weekends; live closer to the office and live in a palace rather than a
flat

**5b**

Well, there are certainly a **few** things I'd like to change. I always seem
to be in a hurry, so it **would** be nice if I had more time. Life would be
much better **if** we had three-day weekends. And I suppose **I** would like
to live closer to my office. Actually no, it would **be** better if I worked
closer to my home. And I'd rather live in a palace than a flat, but
there's not **much** I can do about that. But apart **from** that, I'm pretty
happy with my life!

### Reading

**6a**

A2  B4  C5  D2

**6b**

1 illegal  2 arrested  3 offence  4 forbidden  5 fine

**6c**

1 F  2 T  3 T  4 F

## Lesson 8.2

### Vocabulary | global issues

**1**

1 poverty  2 mortality  3 cure  4 starvation  5 environment  6 standard
7 pollution  8 disease

### Pronunciation | sounds and spelling o

**2**

| Tom | Joe | Paul |
|---|---|---|
| orange | coast | August |
| block | Poland | course |
| cough | home | horse |
| tropical | clothes | waterfalls |
| forests | smoke | boring |
| photographer | overcooks | abroad |

### How to… | express attitude and respond to opinions

**3**

1 right  2 a  3 with  4 luckily  5 that's  6 completely  7 Interestingly
8 off

### Grammar | adverbs

**4**

1 loudly  2 personally  3 unfortunately  4 probably  5 completely
6 clearly  7 really  8 basically

**5**

1 Correct  2 carefully (careful)  3 Correct  4 I don't want definitely
(I definitely don't want)  5 obviously (obvious)  6 Correct  7 Hopeful
(Hopefully)  8 Correct  9 clear (clearly)  10 Correct

### Reading

**6**

1 He went to Uganda.  2 He was a doctor.  3 Yes, he did.

**7**

Correct order: b, e, c, a, d.

## Lesson 8.3

### Grammar | Third Conditional

**1**

1 b  2 a  3 c  4 b  5 a  6 c  7 b  8 c

**2a**

Answers to be confirmed once artwork in place

**2b**

1 hadn't been so much … wouldn't have missed  2 hadn't been …
wouldn't have been able  3 hadn't been … wouldn't have slipped
4 wouldn't have got … 'd taken  5 had realised … would have booked
6 had known … wouldn't have invited

### Pronunciation | sentence stress in Third Conditional

**3a**

1 been/traffic/wouldn't/missed/plane
2 suit/reduced/wouldn't/able/buy
3 hadn't/water/floor/waiter/wouldn't/slipped
4 wouldn't/wet/taken/umbrellas
5 realised/busy/would/booked/table
6 known/already/wouldn't/dinner

### Vocabulary | word building

**4**

1 -ment  2 un-  3 -ence  4 in-  5 -ion  6 over-

**4b**

1 construction  2 difference  3 overcooked  4 unpaid  5 congestion
6 arrangement

### Listening

**5**

Rachel's answers: 1 Her decision was what she should study at
university and what her career would be.  2 She'd always wanted to
be a doctor and she was studying medicine.  3 She didn't like studying
medicine and decided she wanted to change to psychology.
Justin's answers: 1 His decision was about deciding to buy a house
and starting a family.  2 Before that, his work had always been the
most important thing for him.  3 He met Shan and his priorities started
to change.

**6b**

1 twenty-three thousand, nine hundred and ninety-three pounds
2 three-quarters 3 ninety-nine point eight percent 4 the nineteen-nineties 5 the thirtieth of December, two thousand and seven 6 the twentieth century 7 The sixteenth of January, two thousand and eleven 8 two euros twenty (cents)

**How to...** | say numbers
**7a**

1 a 2 b 3 b 4 b 5 a 6 b 7 a 8 b 9 b 10 b

# Lesson 10.3

**Grammar** | phrasal verbs
**1**

1 up 2 through 3 on 4 off 5 up 6 up 7 up 8 on 9 back 10 out

**Pronunciation** | word stress in phrasal verbs
**2**

1 up 2 going 3 on 4 off 5 up 6 up 7 up 8 on 9 back 10 out

**Grammar** | phrasal verbs
**3**

It was great to hear from you again. I've got some good news and some bad news. You remember I told you about my wedding to Maria next month? Well, I'm afraid I've called off it (called it off). Maria and I were going a difficult time through (going through a difficult time). Actually, I don't think she could put up my awful jokes with! (put up with my awful jokes)! But seriously, I think she's already got it over (got over it), and she's already found a new boyfriend! So that's good. You'll never guess who turned at my office up (turned up at my office) the other day. Janet from school! Do you remember her? The one all the boys were in love with! Anyway, I found out she was abroad for a few years, but came last month back (came back last month). So now we work together. And best of all: I'm taking her out to dinner tomorrow night!
Take care and hope to see you soon.
Regards
Tom

**How to...** | say goodbye (in person)
**4**

1 made 2 off 3 coming 4 Have 5 really enjoyed 6 couple 7 see

**Vocabulary** | the senses
**5**

1 e 2 c 3 b 4 a 5 d

**Listening**
**6b**

Correct order: 5, 1, 2, 6, 4, 3

**6c**

1 a 2 b 3 a 4 b 5 b 6 b
**7**

1 a train journey: the woman spends time on train journeys revising vocabulary 2 bed time: the man tried reading his Italian notes at bed time 3 family and friends: the woman practises vocabulary by writing sentences about her family and friends 4 drawing pictures: the woman's friend draws pictures of words and phrases to help her learn them in Japanese 5 language lessons: the woman recommends using new vocabulary in language lessons for practice

# Review and consolidation unit 10

*I wish/If only*
**1**

1 a 2 c 3 a 4 a 5 b 6 b 7 c 8 b
**2**

1 was able to stop 2 hadn't thrown away 3 had bought 4 had taken 5 was able to remember

**Review of past tenses**
**3**

1 was watching 2 didn't go 3 was dancing 4 had left 5 put 6 was trying 7 hadn't seen 8 had taken 10 wasn't staying

**Phrasal verbs**
**4**

1 We called off the picnic/called the picnic off because it was raining. 2 Can you tell me what is going on? 3 You have to come up with a solution. 4 He always turns up late. 5 Climbers can put up with cold weather. 6 I'll find out what happened last night. 7 They're going through a difficult period. 8 When are you planning to come back? 9 They've split up several times before. 10 Carry on running for as long as possible.

**5**

1 found out 2 carry on 3 going through 4 comes back 5 turned up 6 split up 7 put up with 8 come up with 9 call off

**Vocabulary**
**6**

1 b 2 b 3 c 4 a 5 b 6 b 7 c 8 a 9 c 10 a
**7**

1 in 2 from 3 for 4 of 5 against
**8**

1 I wish you **wouldn't** say things like that! 2 She's **widely** considered to be one of the greatest writers in her language. 3 If I'd known, I wouldn't **have** said anything. 4 She turned up **late** again. 5 I'm looking **forward** to seeing you next week. 6 If **only** you would tidy your room more often!

**How to...**
**9**

1 Thanks very **much** for coming. 2 One third is thirty-three **point** three percent. 3 'Taste' rhymes **with** 'raced'. 4 Sorry, I've got **to** dash. 5 I was born on **the** thirtieth of April. 6 It's time I made **a** move. 7 You need to catch the one hundred **and** seven bus to the station. 8 The population of my town is **one/a** hundred thousand. 9 We'll see you in a couple **of** weeks. 10 My Aunt Olive was born in **the** nineteenth century and died in the twenty-first.